Gooseberry Patch
From our Kitchen to Yours

Weeknight Slow Cooker

Table of Contents

Dedication

For every cook who wants to plan simply delicious, low-stress, weekly meals.

....

Appreciation

Thanks to everyone who shared their simple and fun favorite slow-cooker recipes with us!

....

Gooseberry Patch
An imprint of Globe Pequot
246 Goose Lane • Guilford, CT 06437

www.gooseberrypatch.com
1•800•854•6673

Copyright © 2019, Gooseberry Patch
978-1-62093-317-6

Welcome

Dear Friends,

The joy of cooking the slow-cooker way makes weeknight meals better and easier as cooks like you continue to create new recipes to slow-cook and slow-bake, making mealtime so simple.

We love that you can prepare an entire week's menu all from one amazing crock! This cookbook offers over 300 delicious recipes ready to be cooked for you. Just prep and toss your ingredients into your slow cooker, and dinner's done! You'll find simple recipes ready to help out with every after-school menu from snacks, soups and treats to breads, sides and mains. We've even thrown in a few surprise recipes sure to put a smile on your family's faces!

Need something substantial for the kids to snack on before soccer practice or piano lessons? With recipes like Family Favorite Party Mix and Slow-Cooked Scrumptious Salsa, your slow cooker will have yummy before-dinner snacks ready to go. The best meal is a simple meal. With easy-to-fix, hearty and delicious soup, stew and side recipes like Ham & Potato Soup, Zucchini Parmesan or Hearty Carrot Soup, you might be able to sneak in a few vegetables and can rest assured everyone is full and satisfied the rest of the night. It's easy to get a wholesome meal on the table with worry-free recipes like French Country Chicken, Savory Pot Roast and Cheddar Cheese Strata. Surprise your kids and top dinner off with amazing desserts like Apple-Peanut Crumble and Fudgy Pudding Cake. With a special surprise chapter, you'll never have the dinnertime blues. We've added some unexpected ways to cook or bake in your slow cooker. With recipes like Apple-Cinnamon Bread in Jars, Delectable Lemon Cheesecake and Bacon-Wrapped Egg Cups you'll easily add a little "yum!" and fun to any weeknight meal!

So keep dinnertime about family time by taking the hassle out with simple weeknight recipes done the slow-cooker way...you'll be glad dinner's done and so fun. You'll discover the joy of making good food... fast. Enjoy!

Sincerely,
Jo Ann & Vickie

Chapter One

Slow-Cookin' Starters

Starting dinner off right! There are so many ways to kick off weekly meals for family & friends. With tasty starters made in the slow cooker, you can look forward to more time with loved ones and less time in the kitchen. You'll have 'em dancing with yummy dips like Texas Two-Step Dip and juicy and delicious finger foods like Fall-Off-the-Bone Hot Wings. And it may not be pizza night, but add some veggies, or any dippers you can think of, to creamy Pizza Fondue, and everyone will be smiling. Cranberry Meatballs and Cheesy Chicken Ranch Nachos are sure to top off the pre-dinner party in style!

Pizza Fondue

Shannon Finewood, *Corpus Christi, TX*

Pizza Fondue

I make this for fall parties...everyone loves it!

Makes 10 servings

28-oz. jar spaghetti sauce
16-oz. pkg. shredded mozzarella cheese
1/4 c. grated Parmesan cheese
2 T. dried oregano
2 T. dried parsley
1 T. garlic powder
1 t. dried, minced onion
Italian bread cubes, pepperoni chunks, whole
   mushrooms, green pepper slices

Combine sauce, cheeses and seasonings in a slow cooker; mix well. Cover and cook on low setting for 2 hours, or until warmed through and cheese is melted; stir. Serve with desired dippers.

Karen Hazelett, *Fremont, IN*

Girls' Day Delight

Every year, a bunch of friends and I get together for what we call "Girls' Day." It's a weekday that we play hooky from work to relax, catch up, talk about books and eat! We swap lots of recipes, and one year our friend Sherry brought this amazing dip...everyone agreed it was a huge hit!

Serves 10 to 12

14-1/2 oz. can sauerkraut, drained
2 8-oz. pkgs. cream cheese, softened

16-oz. container sour cream
2 8-oz. pkgs. shredded Swiss cheese
3 4-1/2 oz. jars dried beef, diced
1/2 c. milk
crackers or tortilla chips

Combine all ingredients except crackers or chips in a slow cooker; mix well. Cover and cook on high setting, stirring occasionally, for 2 hours, or until mixture is heated through and combined. Serve with crackers or chips for dipping.

Wendy Wright, *New London, WI*

Buttery Mushrooms

My family loves these buttery one-bite mushrooms! So simple and easy. We serve them at all of our get-togethers.

Serves 6

16-oz. pkg. whole mushrooms, trimmed
1/2 c. butter, melted
1-oz. pkg. ranch salad dressing mix

Place mushrooms in a 3-1/2 quart slow cooker. In a small bowl, whisk together butter and salad dressing mix. Pour over mushrooms. Cover and cook on low setting for 3 hours.

Kendall Hale, *Lynn, MA*

Honey-BBQ Chicken Wings

This tasty no-fuss appetizer is a great starter for any occasion.

Serves 4 to 6

3 lbs. chicken wings
salt and pepper to taste
1 c. honey
1/4 c. barbecue sauce
1/4 c. teriyaki sauce
1/4 c. soy sauce
2 T. oil
1 clove garlic, minced
Garnish: green onions, chopped

Arrange chicken wings on a lightly greased broiler pan; sprinkle with salt and pepper. Broil for 12 to 15 minutes on each side, until golden. Transfer wings to a slow cooker. Combine remaining ingredients except garnish in a bowl and pour over wings. Cover and cook on low setting for 4 hours, or on high setting for 2 hours. Garnish with green onions. Serve with sauce from slow cooker.

Amy Thomason Hunt, *Traphill, NC*

Bacon Cheeseburger Dip

All the tastes of a great cheeseburger in one tasty dip!

Serves 10 to 12

6-oz. pkg. real bacon bits, divided
1/2 lb. lean ground beef or turkey
8-oz. pkg. cream cheese, cubed
2 c. shredded Cheddar cheese
10-oz. can diced tomatoes with green chiles
1 t. dried parsley
assorted dippers, such as mini bagel chips,
    tortilla chips and sliced green and red peppers

Reserve 2 tablespoons bacon bits; set aside. In a large skillet over medium heat, brown beef or turkey; drain. Reduce heat to low and stir in cheeses and tomatoes with juice. Cook and stir until heated through. Pour mixture into a 2-quart slow cooker. Cover and cook on low setting for 2 to 3 hours. Before serving, stir in parsley and sprinkle with reserved 2 tablespoons bacon bits. Serve with assorted dippers.

Bacon Cheeseburger Dip

Family Favorite Party Mix

Nola Coons, *Gooseberry Patch*

Family Favorite Party Mix

This snack is always the first to go when I host!

Makes 7 cups

1 c. bite-size crispy wheat cereal squares
1 c. bite-size crispy rice cereal squares
1 c. bite-size crispy corn cereal squares
1 c. peanuts
1 c. pretzel sticks
1/4 c. butter, melted
2 T. Worcestershire sauce
1 t. seasoned salt
1 t. garlic salt
1 c. candy-coated chocolates
1 c. raisins

Combine cereals, nuts and pretzels in a slow cooker. Mix together butter, sauce and salts; gently stir into cereal mixture. Cover and cook on low setting for 3 to 4 hours. Uncover and cook on low setting for an additional 30 minutes; stir occasionally. Drain on paper towel-lined baking sheets; transfer to a large bowl. Cool. Add chocolates and raisins; toss to mix. Store in an airtight container.

Rhonda Weaver, *Leechburg, PA*

Game-Day Dip

My son requests this weekly when we watch our favorite Pittsburgh football team. Sunday is all about the four "F's" in our house...family, football, food and fun! Try different flavors of diced tomatoes to mix up the flavor.

Serves 6 to 8

1-1/2 lbs. ground beef
1 to 2 cloves garlic, minced
salt and pepper to taste
14-1/2 oz. can petite diced tomatoes, drained
18-oz. bottle hickory barbecue sauce
tortilla chips

Brown beef and garlic in a skillet over medium heat; season with salt and pepper. Drain and spoon beef mixture into a slow cooker. Add remaining ingredients except chips to beef mixture; mix well. Cover and cook on low setting for 2 to 3 hours, until heated through and thickened. Serve with tortilla chips for dipping.

Whitney Burgess, *Florence, AL*

Party Corn Dip

This is my go-to recipe for any party. It's so simple, fast and always a crowd-pleaser!

Serves 8 to 10

3 15-oz. cans shoepeg corn
3 10-oz. cans diced tomatoes with green chiles
3 8-oz. pkgs. cream cheese, cubed
corn chips

Partially drain each can of corn and tomatoes, leaving about half the liquid in each can. Pour corn and tomatoes with remaining liquid into a slow cooker; add cream cheese. Cover and cook on low setting for one to 2 hours, stirring occasionally, until cream cheese is melted and dip is warmed through. Serve warm with corn chips for dipping.

Jewel Sharpe, Raleigh, NC

Sticks & Stones

A delicious and festive party appetizer...there are never any leftovers at our get-togethers!

Serves 12 to 16

14-oz. Kielbasa sausage ring, cut into bite-size
   pieces
32-oz. pkg. frozen mini meatballs, thawed
10-oz. jar currant jelly
10-oz. jar red pepper jelly
1 T. Dijon mustard
pretzel sticks or toothpicks

Add sausage and meatballs to a slow cooker. In a microwave-safe bowl, combine jellies and mustard; microwave on high setting until mixture is melted and well blended. Pour hot jelly mixture over kielbasa and meatballs. Cover and cook on low setting for one to 2 hours, until heated through. Serve with pretzel sticks or toothpicks.

Debra Collins, Gaylesville, AL

Cheesy Sausage Dip

This is an awesome dip for any party!

Serves 10 to 15

1 lb. ground pork sausage
8-oz. pkg. cream cheese, cubed
8-oz. container sour cream
10-oz. can diced tomatoes with green chiles
1 c. shredded Cheddar cheese
10-oz. pkg. frozen spinach, thawed and drained
1/2 t. garlic powder

In a skillet over medium heat, brown sausage; drain and set aside. In a slow cooker, combine cream cheese, sour cream, tomatoes with juice and Cheddar cheese. Cover and cook on low setting for one hour, or until cheeses are melted. Stir in spinach, sausage and garlic powder. Cover and cook on low setting for one to 2 hours longer, until dip is smooth and warmed through.

Tanya Miller, Millersburg, OH

Creamy Hot Corn Dip

No one can resist this creamy, yummy dip.

Makes 15 servings

2 8-oz. pkgs. cream cheese, softened
2 15-1/4 oz. cans corn, drained
1/2 c. butter
2 jalapeño peppers, diced
tortilla chips

Combine all ingredients except tortilla chips in a slow cooker. Cover and cook on high setting for 30 minutes; stir until smooth. Reduce setting to low to keep warm. The longer it cooks, the spicier it will get. Serve with tortilla chips.

Creamy Hot Corn Dip

Amazing Brie Fondue

Vivian Long, *Columbus, OH*

Amazing Brie Fondue

I make this rich fondue for all holidays and special events. It disappears quickly...I usually have to make at least a double batch! Spread some on a toasted baguette slice, top with cinnamon, red pepper flakes, herbs and crumbled sausage. It is also great drizzled over fresh and steamed vegetables, or used as a sauce for pasta dishes!

Serves 6 to 8

8-oz. brie cheese round, rind removed
8-oz. pkg. cream cheese, cubed
1 c. butter, sliced

Cut brie into chunks. Combine all ingredients in a small slow cooker. Cover and cook on low setting for one hour, stirring occasionally, until all ingredients are blended and smooth. Be careful not to let fondue come to a boil. If slow cooker gets too hot, turn it off for about 5 to 8 minutes.

Carolyn Deckard, *Bedford, IN*

Crockery Party Mix

We have made this party mix for years to give as gifts for our neighbors, friends, papergirl and mailman. We buy plastic jars that have green or red lids. To add a little color we use strips of Christmas fabric to tie around the lid. Sometimes we add an ornament...cute!

Serves 10 to 12

3 c. thin pretzel sticks
2 c. bite-size crispy wheat cereal
2 c. bite-size crispy rice cereal
2 c. doughnut-shaped oat cereal
2 c. dry-roasted peanuts
1 t. celery salt
1 t. garlic salt
1/2 t. salt
2 T. grated Parmesan cheese
1/2 c. butter, melted

In a large bowl, combine pretzels, cereal and peanuts. Sprinkle with seasonings and cheese; drizzle with butter. Toss lightly. Transfer mixture to a large slow cooker. Cover and cook on low setting for 3-1/2 hours. Uncover and cook 30 minutes longer, stirring occasionally. Serve immediately, or store in airtight containers.

Heather Eldredge, *Langhorne, PA*

Grammam Phyllis's Italian Meatballs

Serve as an appetizer, or ladle over cooked spaghetti for a hearty meal.

Serves 6 to 8

1 lb. ground beef
1/2 c. Italian-flavored dry bread crumbs
1 t. grated Parmesan cheese
2 eggs, beaten
3 26-oz. jars favorite spaghetti sauce
Optional: 16-oz. pkg. spaghetti, uncooked

In a large bowl, combine beef, bread crumbs, cheese and eggs; mix well. Form beef mixture into one-inch balls. Place meatballs in a slow cooker; cover with sauce. Cover and cook on low setting for 8 to 10 hours. About 15 minutes before serving, prepare spaghetti according to package directions; drain. Ladle sauce and meatballs over individual servings of spaghetti.

Rogene Rogers, *Bemidji, MN*

Hot Broccoli Cheese Dip

You'll see the crock bottom before halftime with this cheesy dip!

Makes 10 to 12 servings

3/4 c. butter
3 stalks celery, thinly sliced
1 onion, chopped
4-oz. can sliced mushrooms, drained
3 T. all-purpose flour
10-3/4 oz. can cream of celery soup
3 c. shredded Cheddar cheese
10-oz. pkg. frozen chopped broccoli, thawed

Melt butter in a skillet over medium heat; sauté celery, onion and mushrooms. Stir in flour; mix well. Transfer mixture to a lightly greased slow cooker; mix in remaining ingredients. Cover and cook on high setting until cheese is melted, stirring every 15 minutes. Continue cooking, covered, on low setting for 2 to 4 hours.

Hot Broccoli Cheese Dip

Crabby Artichoke Spread

Kathy Grashoff, *Fort Wayne, IN*

Crabby Artichoke Spread

Your guests will just love this creamy, spicy dip!

Makes 3 to 4 cups

1 jalapeño pepper, seeded and chopped
1 t. oil
14-oz. can artichokes, drained and chopped
2 6-oz. cans crabmeat, drained
1 c. mayonnaise
1/2 red pepper, chopped
1/2 c. grated Parmesan cheese
2 green onions, chopped
2 t. lemon juice
2 t. Worcestershire sauce
1/2 t. celery seed
toasted bread rounds or crackers

Sauté jalapeño in oil until tender. Combine jalapeño and remaining ingredients except bread rounds or crackers in a slow-cooker. Cover and cook on low setting for 4 hours. Serve with bread rounds or crackers.

Zoe Bennett, *Columbia, SC*

Simply Scrumptious Sticky Wings

Get out the napkins, because these delectable treats are as messy as they are tasty. The ginger really adds a nice zip to the sauce...we love to have a big plate of these on game days.

Makes 8 servings

3/4 c. dark brown sugar, packed and divided
1/4 c. soy sauce, divided
4 cloves garlic, minced
2 T. fresh ginger, minced
1/2 t. cayenne pepper, divided
4 lbs. chicken wings
salt and pepper to taste
1/4 c. water
1/4 c. tomato paste

Combine 1/4 cup brown sugar, one tablespoon soy sauce, garlic, ginger and 1/4 teaspoon cayenne pepper in a slow cooker. Season chicken wings with salt and pepper; add to sugar mixture. Toss wings to coat well. Cover and cook on low setting for 4 to 5 hours, until chicken is tender and no longer pink in the center. Remove wings to a rack on an aluminum foil-lined baking sheet; set aside. In a bowl, combine remaining brown sugar, soy sauce and cayenne pepper, water and tomato paste; mix well. Brush wings with half of sauce. Broil wings until crisp on one side, about 10 minutes. Turn wings and brush with remaining sauce; broil until other side is crisp, about 5 minutes.

Lynnette Jones, East Flat Rock, NC

Mapley Appetizers

With traditional Christmas colors from the green pepper and the red maraschino cherries, this is a wonderful holiday appetizer. The recipe was passed down to me by my husband's aunt.

Serves 8 to 10

15-1/4 oz. can pineapple tidbits, drained and
   juice reserved
1/2 c. maple syrup
1/2 c. vinegar
1/3 c. water
4 t. cornstarch
14-oz. pkg. mini smoked sausages
2/3 c. green pepper, cut into 1-inch squares
1/2 c. maraschino cherries

In a bowl, blend reserved pineapple juice, maple syrup, vinegar and water; stir in cornstarch. Pour into a slow cooker. Add pineapple and remaining ingredients; stir gently. Cover and cook on low setting for 4 to 6 hours.

Kerry Mayer, Dunham Springs, LA

Cajun Spiced Pecans

A great snack to take to a party. You can even share with individual treat bags.

12 to 16 servings

16-oz. pkg. pecan halves
1/4 c. butter, melted
1 T. chili powder
1 t. dried basil
1 t. dried oregano
1 t. dried thyme
1 t. salt
1/2 t. onion powder
1/4 t. garlic powder
1/4 t. cayenne pepper

Combine all ingredients in a slow cooker. Cover and cook on high setting for 15 minutes. Turn to low setting and cook, uncovered, for 2 hours, stirring occasionally. Transfer nuts to a baking sheet; cool completely. Store in an airtight container.

Cajun Spiced Pecans

Brittney Green, *Frederick, CO*

Aunt Barb's Dip

This dip has been a favorite in our family for years...everyone just loves it! It's perfect for fall football parties. You can easily double the recipe, and you very well may need to.

Serves 20

1-1/2 lbs. ground beef
1 onion, chopped
1 green pepper, chopped
1 T. chili powder
14-1/2 oz. can stewed tomatoes
15-oz. can ranch-style pinto beans with
   jalapeños
10-3/4 oz. can cream of chicken soup
10-3/4 oz. can cream of mushroom soup
16-oz. pkg. pasteurized process cheese spread,
   cubed
tortilla chips

In a skillet over medium heat, brown beef with onion and green pepper; drain. Sprinkle with chili powder. Transfer beef mixture to a large slow cooker; add undrained tomatoes, undrained beans and remaining ingredients except tortilla chips. Stir well. Cover and cook on low setting for 4 hours, stirring occasionally, until cheese melts and dip is warmed through. Serve warm with tortilla chips.

Kim Ralston, *Murfreesboro, TN*

Kimmy's Amazing Black Bean Chili-Cheese Dip

This festive dip is my go-to dip for any get-together! It freezes wonderfully too, so you can make it in advance.

Serves 24

1 lb. ground beef
1 lb. ground pork sausage
32-oz. pkg. pasteurized process cheese spread,
   cubed
8-oz. pkg. cream cheese, cubed
2 15-1/2 oz. cans black beans, drained and rinsed
3 14-1/2 oz. cans fire-roasted diced tomatoes
6 T. taco seasoning mix
1-oz. pkg. fiesta ranch dip mix
assorted dippers, such as tortilla chips, corn
   chips and cut veggies

In a skillet over medium heat, brown beef and sausage until crumbled and no longer pink; drain. To a 6 to 7-quart slow cooker, add cheeses, beans and tomatoes with juice. Add beef mixture. Sprinkle with seasoning mixes; stir well. Cover and cook on low setting for 2 hours, stirring every 20 minutes, until cheeses are melted and dip is warmed through. Turn slow cooker to warm setting; serve with dippers.

Kimmy's Amazing Black Bean Chili-Cheese Dip

Seaside Crab Dip

Lisa Columbo, Appleton, WI

Seaside Crab Dip

This dip is easy to make and loved even by the pickiest of eaters.

Makes 24 servings

2 8-oz. pkgs. cream cheese
3 T. butter
1 bunch green onions, chopped
1 lb. crabmeat, flaked or chopped
onion and garlic salt to taste
garlic melba toast

In a microwave-safe bowl, mix all ingredients together except melba toast. Microwave on high setting until warm. Pour into a slow cooker; cover and keep warm on low setting. Serve with melba toast.

Lynn Williams, Muncie, IN

Soy & Honey Chicken Wings

A must at our family's annual holiday get-together!

Serves 6 to 8

3 lbs. chicken wings
salt and pepper to taste
1-1/2 c. honey
1/2 c. soy sauce
2 T. oil
2 T. catsup
1 clove garlic, minced

Season wings with salt and pepper. Place wings in a lightly greased large slow cooker. In a bowl, combine remaining ingredients; mix well and pour evenly over wings. Cover and cook on low setting for 6 to 8 hours, until wings are glazed and chicken juices run clear when pierced.

Jennifer Crisp, Abingdon, IL

Pleasing Pizza Dip

This recipe goes so fast that I have to put out two slow cookers for our family gatherings! You can toss in any of your favorite pizza toppings, and it will be delicious.

Serves 10 to 12

1 c. ground Italian pork sausage, browned and
   drained
1 c. pepperoni, diced
2 8-oz. pkgs. cream cheese, cubed
2 c. shredded Cheddar cheese
1-1/2 c. sour cream
2-1/2 c. pizza sauce
2 to 3 T. dried oregano
2 t. garlic powder
tortilla chips

Combine all ingredients except tortilla chips in a slow cooker. Cover and cook on low setting for 2 hours, stirring occasionally, until dip is smooth and warmed through. Serve warm with tortilla chips.

Jessica Kraus, Delaware, OH

Spinach Queso Dip

This is the perfect dip for football season. Creamy queso and bright spinach is a flavor combination that's always a winner.

Serves 10

1 lb. Mexican-style pasteurized process cheese spread, cubed
10-oz. pkg. frozen chopped spinach, thawed and drained well
16-oz. container salsa
8-oz. pkg. cream cheese, cubed
Optional: chopped fresh cilantro
tortilla chips

Combine all ingredients except cilantro and tortilla chips in a slow cooker. Cover and cook on high setting for one to 2 hours, stirring occasionally, until cheeses are melted. Turn heat to low setting to keep warm. Stir in cilantro just before serving; serve with chips for dipping.

~ *Handy Tip* ~

A bag of tortilla chips, a jar of salsa, some brightly colored lanterns, paper flowers and maracas make a complete fiesta for sharing with roommates!

Jo Ann, Gooseberry Patch

Rosemary-White Bean Dip

Rosemary is one of my favorite herbs, so I always have a couple pots of it growing on my windowsill. A good friend shared this recipe with me, and I just knew I had to try it. So one game day I whipped up a batch, and was it a hit!

Serves 4 to 6

3/4 c. dried white beans
4 cloves garlic, minced
1 T. fresh rosemary, chopped
1 t. red pepper flakes
2 c. vegetable broth
salt to taste
7 T. olive oil
1-1/2 T. lemon juice
1 T. fresh parsley, chopped
assorted dippers such as crackers, toasted baguette slices and cherry tomatoes

Combine beans, garlic, rosemary, pepper flakes and broth in a medium slow cooker. Cover and cook on high setting for 3 hours, or until beans are soft and liquid is mostly absorbed. Remove crock and cool. Place cooled bean mixture into a blender; stir in oil and lemon juice. Process until dip reaches desired consistency. Spoon dip into a serving bowl; sprinkle with parsley. Serve with dippers.

Rosemary-White Bean Dip

Darrell Lawry, *Kissimmee, FL*

Firecracker Party Mix

This party mix is a staple on my game-day potluck table. It seems like it's always the first to go. It has a delicious savory-hot flavor that guests just keep coming back for.

Makes about 15 cups

8 c. popped popcorn
4 c. bite-size crispy corn cereal squares
3 c. pretzel sticks
1/4 c. Worcestershire sauce
1/4 c. butter, melted
2 T. brown sugar, packed
1-1/2 t. salt
1/2 t. cayenne pepper

Combine popcorn, cereal and pretzels in a slow cooker; set aside. In a bowl, mix together sauce, butter, brown sugar, salt and pepper. Drizzle sauce mixture over popcorn mixture, stirring well to coat evenly. Cover and cook on low setting for 2 to 3 hours. Remove lid and cook on low setting for one more hour. Spoon party mix onto a baking sheet to cool. Serve, or store in an airtight container. Will keep for about one week.

Jennie Growden, *Cumberland, MD*

Fall-Off-the-Bone Hot Wings

This recipe was born out of my love for two things...chicken wings and quick & easy recipes.

Serves 10 to 15

4 to 5 lbs. chicken wings
seafood seasoning to taste
12-oz. bottle cayenne hot pepper sauce
3 T. butter

Place wings on an aluminum foil-lined baking sheet; sprinkle with seafood seasoning. Bake at 325 degrees for 30 minutes. Sprinkle wings with a little hot sauce; flip wings over and sprinkle with sauce again. Bake for an additional 30 minutes. Combine wings, remaining hot sauce and butter in a slow cooker. Cover and cook on high setting for one hour; reduce heat to low setting and cook for 2 to 3 hours more.

Beth Bennett, *Stratham, NH*

Hot Tomato-Cheese Dip

The mushroom soup is the "secret" ingredient... it really makes a difference.

Serves 10 to 12

16-oz. pkg. pasteurized process cheese spread,
    cubed
10-oz. can diced tomatoes with green chiles
10-3/4 oz. can cream of mushroom soup
assorted dippers, such as corn chips or sliced
    veggies

Combine all ingredients except dippers in a slow cooker. Cover and cook on low setting for one to 2 hours, until dip is smooth and warmed through. Serve warm with corn chips or veggies for dipping.

Kimberly Hancock, *Murrieta, CA*

Honey Sesame Wings

These wings are mild, but zesty enough to please everyone.

Makes about 2-1/2 dozen

3 lbs. chicken wings
salt and pepper to taste
2 c. honey
1 c. soy sauce
1/2 c. catsup
1/4 c. oil
2 cloves garlic, minced
Garnish: sesame seed

Place chicken wings on an ungreased broiler pan; sprinkle with salt and pepper. Place pan 4 to 5 inches under broiler. Broil for 10 minutes on each side, or until chicken is golden. Transfer wings to a slow cooker. Combine remaining ingredients except sesame seed; pour over wings. Cover and cook on low setting for 4 to 5 hours, or high setting for 2 to 2-1/2 hours. Arrange on a serving platter; sprinkle with sesame seed.

Honey Sesame Wings

Lesleigh Robinson, *Brownsville, TN*

Cranberry Meatballs

This is a great appetizer for Christmas or anytime.

Serves 10 to 12

28-oz. pkg. frozen meatballs
2 3/4-oz. pkgs. brown gravy mix
2 14-oz. cans whole-berry cranberry sauce
2 T. whipping cream
2 t. Dijon mustard
2 18-oz. bottles barbecue sauce

Place meatballs in a slow cooker. In a bowl, prepare gravy mixes according to package directions; stir in cranberry sauce, cream and mustard. Pour over meatballs; stir. Cover and cook on low setting for 4 to 5 hours, or on high setting for 2 to 3 hours. Before serving, drain gravy mixture; return meatballs to slow cooker to keep warm. Stir in barbecue sauce.

Patricia Stagich, *Elizabeth, NJ*

Club Sandwich Dip

I like to serve this tasty dip with rye toast points...just like a good deli sandwich!

Serves 20

1 lb. deli turkey, chopped
1/2 lb. deli ham, chopped
1/2 lb. sliced Swiss or American cheese, chopped
8-oz. pkg. cream cheese, cubed
1 c. mayonnaise
2 t. Dijon mustard
6 slices bacon, crisply cooked and crumbled
1/2 c. cherry or grape tomatoes, chopped
toast points and assorted cut veggies

In a 4-quart slow cooker, combine turkey, ham, cheeses, mayonnaise and mustard. Cover and cook on high setting for one to 2 hours, until cheeses are melted, stirring after one hour. Before serving, stir in half of the bacon; garnish with remaining bacon and tomatoes. Serve warm with toast points and veggies.

Club Sandwich Dip

Chunky Applesauce

Lisa Ann Panzino-DiNunzio, *Vineland, NJ*

Chunky Applesauce

There's nothing like homemade applesauce, and it can't get any easier than this yummy recipe!

Makes 6 to 8 servings

10 apples, peeled, cored and cubed
1/2 c. water
3/4 c. sugar
Optional: 1 t. cinnamon

Combine all ingredients in a slow cooker; toss to mix. Cover and cook on low setting for 8 to 10 hours. Serve warm or keep refrigerated in a covered container.

Beckie Apple, *Grannis, AR*

BBQ Mustard Pigs

Game-day snacks are a big part of setting the winning mood at our house. This one is easy and always a favorite.

Serves 6

1 lb. mini smoked sausages
1/4 c. spicy brown mustard
2 c. barbecue sauce
1 c. grape jelly
1 T. smoke-flavored cooking sauce

Combine all ingredients in a slow cooker. Cover and cook on high setting for one to 2 hours, until sausages are heated through and sauce is thickened.

Amy Shilliday, *San Antonio, TX*

Texas Queso Dip

The hot pork in this dip really spices things up!

Makes 10 to 12 servings

1 lb. hot ground pork sausage, browned and
 drained
32-oz. pkg. pasteurized process cheese spread,
 cubed
10-oz. can diced tomatoes with green chiles
1/2 c. milk
white corn tortilla chips

Combine all ingredients except tortilla chips in a slow cooker. Cover and cook on low setting until cheese is melted, about 2 hours. Serve with tortilla chips.

Regina Vining, *Warwick, RI*

Ginger Thai Wings

These wings have a very unique, finger-licking flavor that you can't find anywhere else. I set a plate of them out while the game's on, and before I know it, they're gone.

Serves 12

2-1/4 lbs. chicken wings
3/4 c. water, divided
1 T. lime juice
3/4 t. ground ginger, divided
1/2 c. creamy peanut butter
2 T. soy sauce
2 cloves garlic, minced
1/4 t. red pepper flakes

Place wings in a slow cooker. Add 1/4 cup water, lime juice and 1/4 teaspoon ginger to wings; stir to coat well. Cover and cook on low setting for 5 to 6 hours. Meanwhile, whisk together peanut butter, remaining water, remaining ginger and other ingredients in a small saucepan over medium heat. Cook, whisking constantly, until mixture is smooth. Remove wings to a serving bowl. Drizzle peanut sauce over wings. Toss to coat well.

Cheryl Volbruck, *Costa Mesa, CA*

All-Day Apple Butter

This homemade treat is fun to make and fills the house with a delicious aroma.

Makes 5 to 6 jars

3-1/2 lbs. Pippin apples, peeled, cored and sliced
2 lbs. Granny Smith apples, peeled, cored and sliced
2 c. sugar
2 c. brown sugar, packed
2 t. cinnamon
1/4 t. ground cloves
1/4 t. salt
1/8 t. nutmeg
6 1/2-pt. canning jars and lids, sterilized

Place all ingredients in a large slow cooker. Stir to mix well. Cover and cook on high setting for one hour. Reduce heat to low setting and cook 9 to 11 hours more, stirring occasionally, until mixture is thick and dark brown. Uncover; cook one hour longer. Ladle hot butter into hot sterilized jars, leaving 1/4-inch headspace. Wipe rims; secure with lids and rings. Process in a boiling water bath for 10 minutes. Set jars on a towel to cool; check for seals.

All-Day Apple Butter

Italian Scallion Meatballs

Wendy Jacobs, *Idaho Falls, ID*

Italian Scallion Meatballs

I love to use themed toothpicks to serve these.

Makes about 11 dozen

1 c. grape juice
1 c. apple jelly
1 c. catsup
8-oz. can tomato sauce
4 lbs. frozen Italian-style meatballs
Garnish: sliced green onions

In a small saucepan, combine all ingredients except meatballs and garnish. Cook and stir over medium heat until jelly is melted; remove from heat. Place meatballs in a slow cooker; pour sauce over top and gently stir to coat. Cover and cook on low setting for 4 hours. Sprinkle with onions at serving time.

Connie Bryant, *Topeka, KS*

Spicy Apricot-Pear Chutney

A spicy-sweet treat perfect on toast or English muffins, or serve with cocktail sausages for dipping.

Makes about 7 cups

6 pears, cored and diced
2 c. dried apricots, chopped
1/4 c. green onion, sliced
1/4 c. lemon juice
2 c. sugar
2 t. lemon zest
1/2 t. red pepper flakes

Combine all ingredients in a slow cooker. Cover and cook on low setting for 3 to 4 hours, until pears are tender and sauce has thickened. Spoon into covered containers and refrigerate for up to 2 weeks.

~ *Handy Tip* ~

A new terra cotta pot makes a terrific ice bucket. Simply line the pot with wax paper, fill with ice and add a new garden trowel.

Susan Paffenroth, *Johnson City, TN*

Susie's Make-Ahead Doggy Dogs

A simple appetizer that everyone's sure to love. Try using turkey or chicken hot dogs too.

Serves 12 to 15

3 16-oz. pkgs. hot dogs, sliced into 1-inch pieces
18-oz. bottle barbecue sauce
20-oz. can pineapple chunks, drained and juice reserved
1/2 c. brown sugar, packed
1/4 c. apple jelly
1/4 c. grape jelly

Place hot dogs in a slow cooker; set aside. In a saucepan over medium-low heat, combine barbecue sauce, reserved pineapple juice, brown sugar and jellies. Heat, stirring occasionally, until warmed and combined. Add pineapple chunks to hot dogs in slow cooker; spoon sauce over all. Cover and cook on low setting for 3 hours, or until heated through.

Rebecca Done, *San Antonio, TX*

Spicy White Cheese Dip

This crowd-pleaser gets its kick from canned diced tomatoes with green chiles.

Makes about 8 cups

2 lbs. white American deli cheese slices, torn
1/2 c. onion, finely chopped
1 t. garlic, minced
2 10-oz. cans diced tomatoes with green chiles
3/4 c. milk
1/2 t. ground cumin
1/2 t. coarsely ground pepper
assorted chips

Place all ingredients, except chips, in a 6-quart slow cooker. Cover and cook on low setting for 3 hours, stirring gently every hour. Adjust slow cooker setting to warm. Stir before serving. Serve with assorted chips.

~ *Handy Tip* ~

A vintage muffin tin is perfect for serving a variety of savory dips and spreads. Just spoon a different flavor into each muffin cup.

Spicy White Cheese Dip

Holiday Chutney

Megan Brooks, Antioch, TN

Holiday Chutney

Delicious with roast pork, or for a delicious party snack, spoon chutney over a brick of cream cheese. Serve with crackers.

Makes about 2-1/2 cups

2 c. tart apples, peeled, cored and chopped
1/2 c. golden raisins
1/2 c. honey
3 T. cider vinegar
1/2 t. ground ginger
1/2 t. dry mustard
1/2 t. curry powder
1/4 t. salt

Combine apples and raisins in a mini slow cooker. Stir together remaining ingredients in a small bowl; pour over fruit mixture and stir. Cover and cook on low setting for 6 hours. Cool; spoon into a covered container.

Melissa Flasck, Sterling Heights, MI

Cheesy Chicken Ranch Nachos

Great for working moms. It's quick & easy to toss together in the morning and gives me more time to play with my son!

Serves 4

1-1/2 lbs. boneless, skinless chicken breasts or thighs
2 10-3/4 oz. cans Cheddar cheese soup
1-1/2 c. chicken broth
1 c. salsa
15-1/4 oz. can corn, drained
tortilla chips
Garnish: ranch salad dressing
Optional: extra salsa or hot pepper sauce

Place chicken in a slow cooker; top with soup and salsa. Cover and cook on low setting for 8 hours, or on high setting for 4 hours. Add corn in the last 30 minutes of cooking. Shred chicken with 2 forks and return to slow cooker. To serve, cover dinner plates with tortilla chips; ladle chicken mixture over chips and drizzle with salad dressing. Top with salsa or hot sauce, if desired.

Marlene Darnell, Newport Beach, CA

Tuscan White Bean Spread

This savory, healthy spread is sure to be welcome at your next holiday get-together.

Serves 10 to 12

4 15-oz. cans cannellini beans, drained and rinsed
1 onion, chopped
4 cloves garlic, chopped
2 T. extra-virgin olive oil
1 c. water
1 t. dried rosemary
1 t. red pepper flakes
1 t. salt
1 t. pepper
crostini slices

Combine all ingredients in a slow cooker; stir. Cover and cook on high setting for 3 hours, or on low setting for 5 hours. Serve warm with crostini.

Donna Lewis, *Ostrander, OH*

Buffalo Chicken Dip

It just wouldn't be a party without everyone's favorite dip!

Serves 10 to 12

2 8-oz. pkgs. cream cheese, cubed
1 c. ranch salad dressing
1 c. buffalo wing sauce
3 boneless, skinless chicken breasts,
    cooked and shredded
1 c. shredded Mexican-blend cheese
tortilla chips

In a slow cooker, combine cream cheese, salad dressing and wing sauce. Cover and cook on high setting for one to 2 hours. When cream cheese is melted and mixture is creamy, stir in chicken and shredded cheese. Cover and cook until heated through. Before serving, turn slow cooker to low setting. Serve warm with tortilla chips.

Lori Roggenbuck, *Ubly, MI*

Bacon-Double Cheese Dip

Bacon makes everything better!

Serves 10 to 12

8 slices bacon, chopped
2 8-oz. pkgs. cream cheese, softened
1 c. mayonnaise
8-oz. pkg. shredded Swiss cheese
8-oz. pkg. shredded Cheddar cheese
2 green onions, finely chopped
crackers, sliced assorted vegetables

Crisply cook bacon in a skillet over medium heat; drain and set aside. In a bowl, beat cream cheese and mayonnaise until smooth. Stir in Swiss and Cheddar cheeses, green onions and cooked bacon, reserving a little bacon for topping. Spoon dip mixture into a slow cooker. Cover and cook on low setting for 3 hours, or until hot and smooth. Garnish dip with reserved cooked bacon. Serve with crackers and vegetables for dipping.

Bacon-Double Cheese Dip

Marlene Darnell, *Newport Beach, CA*

Slow-Cooked Scrumptious Salsa

Making your own salsa is so fresh & good!

Makes about 2 cups

10 roma tomatoes, cored
2 cloves garlic
1 onion, cut into wedges
2 jalapeño peppers, seeded and chopped
1/4 c. fresh cilantro, coarsely chopped
1/2 t. salt

Combine tomatoes, garlic and onion in a slow cooker. Cover and cook on high setting for 2-1/2 to 3 hours, until vegetables are tender. Remove crock and let cool. Combine cooled tomato mixture and remaining ingredients in a food processor or blender. Process to desired consistency. May be refrigerated in a covered container for about one week.

Karen Hazelett, *Fremont, IN*

Slow-Cooker Pub Dip

Serve with pretzels, crackers or sliced vegetables.

Makes about 4 cups

2 5-oz. jars sharp Cheddar cheese spread
8-oz. pkg. cream cheese, softened
1/2 c. regular or non-alcoholic beer
1 t. Worcestershire sauce
5 to 6 drops hot pepper sauce
4 to 5 slices bacon, crisply cooked and crumbled
pretzels, crackers or sliced vegetables

Combine cheeses, beer and sauces in a greased 2-1/2 to 3-quart slow cooker. Cover and cook on low setting 2 hours, stirring occasionally; the dip will become thicker the longer it cooks. Stir in bacon just before serving, sprinkling some on top. Serve with pretzels, crackers or vegetables.

Karen Schmidt, *Racine, WI*

Hot Crab Rangoon Dip

This is so easy to mix up for a party, and it always brings loads of compliments.

Serves 10 to 12

2 8-oz. pkgs. cream cheese, softened
2 6-oz. cans crabmeat, drained and flaked
10-3/4 oz. can cream of shrimp soup
1 T. green onion, finely chopped
1 t. lemon juice
2 t. soy sauce
1 t. Worcestershire sauce
rice crackers

Combine all ingredients except crackers in a 3 to 4-quart slow cooker; mix well. Cover and cook on low setting for 2 to 3 hours. Serve with crackers.

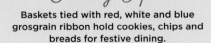

~ *Handy Tip* ~

Baskets tied with red, white and blue grosgrain ribbon hold cookies, chips and breads for festive dining.

Thomas Campbell, *Eden Prairie, MN*

Italian Mushrooms

These are so easy to make, they practically cook themselves!

Serves 8 to 10

4 lbs. small whole mushrooms, trimmed
2 c. butter, cut into thirds
0.7-oz. pkg. regular or zesty Italian salad
   dressing mix

Place mushrooms in a slow cooker; top with butter and seasoning mix. Cover and cook on high setting for 3 to 4 hours, stirring occasionally. Turn slow cooker to low setting to keep mushrooms warm. Serve with toothpicks.

Gina LiVolsi Norton, *Wonder Lake, IL*

World's Best Cocktail Meatballs

This recipe has been in our family for over 50 years. They are the best cocktail meatballs anyone has ever tasted. Just set out a crock of these and watch them disappear...enjoy!

Serves 10

1 lb. ground beef chuck
1/2 c. corn flake cereal, crushed
1/2 c. evaporated milk
12-oz. bottle chili sauce, divided
1 T. Worcestershire sauce
1/4 c. onion, finely chopped
1 t. salt
10-oz. jar grape jelly

In a bowl, combine beef, cereal, milk, 1/4 cup chili sauce, Worcestershire sauce, onion and salt; mix well. Cover and refrigerate for 30 minutes. Form beef mixture into walnut-size balls. Place meatballs on a baking sheet; bake at 375 degrees for 20 minutes, or until browned. Transfer meatballs to a slow cooker; set aside. In a saucepan over medium heat, combine remaining chili sauce and grape jelly. Cook and stir until jelly is melted; spoon over meatballs and stir gently. Set slow cooker to low setting for serving; heat through.

Rachel Adams, *Fort Lewis, WA*

Spinach-Artichoke Dip

My family flips for this veggie-packed dip.

Serves 10 to 12

14-oz. can artichoke hearts, drained and
    chopped
2 bunches fresh spinach, chopped
2 8-oz. pkgs. reduced-fat cream cheese, softened
    and cubed
2-1/2 c. shredded Monterey Jack cheese
2-1/2 c. shredded mozzarella cheese
3 cloves garlic, minced
1/4 t. pepper
pita chips and assorted sliced vegetables
    for dipping

Combine chopped artichokes, spinach and cheeses in a slow cooker; mix well. Stir in garlic and pepper. Cover and cook on high setting for about one to 2 hours, stirring occasionally, until cheeses are melted and dip is smooth. Reduce heat to low setting to keep warm. Serve with pita chips and sliced vegetables for dipping.

~ *Handy tip* ~

Arrange baby veggies in a cornucopia basket for dipping! Cherry tomatoes, snow peas, baby corn and mini mushrooms are all pleasing to the eye and to the tastebuds.

Spinach-Artichoke Dip

Buffalo Chicken Potato Skins

Melanie Lowe, *Dover, DE*

Buffalo Chicken Potato Skins

These are perfect for tailgating parties.

Serves 6 to 8

1 lb. boneless, skinless chicken breasts
1/2 onion, chopped
1 clove garlic, minced
1 stalk celery, chopped
14-1/2 oz. can chicken broth
1/3 c. cayenne hot pepper sauce
6 baking potatoes, baked
salt and pepper to taste
3/4 c. shredded Cheddar cheese
Garnish: blue cheese salad dressing

Combine chicken, onion, garlic, celery and broth in a slow cooker. Cover and cook on high setting for 4 hours, or until chicken is no longer pink in the center. Remove and shred chicken, reserving 1/2 cup juices from slow cooker, discarding the rest. Combine shredded chicken, reserved broth and hot sauce in slow cooker. Cover and cook on high setting for 30 minutes. Meanwhile, slice potatoes in half lengthwise; scoop out pulp and save for another recipe. Place potato skins on a lightly greased baking sheet. Lightly spray skins with non-stick vegetable spray; sprinkle with salt and pepper. Bake at 450 degrees for 10 minutes, or until lightly golden. Evenly divide chicken mixture and Cheddar cheese among potato skins. Bake again for about 5 minutes, or until cheese is melted. Drizzle potatoes with dressing before serving.

Renee Bailey, *Tomah, WI*

Game-Day Sausage Rolls

My mom always made this game-day favorite, and it's still a favorite with my family today! It's a perfect sandwich to enjoy on those cool-weather football Sundays.

Makes 12 servings

6 smoked pork bratwursts, cut into thirds
6 smoked hot Italian pork sausages, cut into thirds
1 onion, sliced
1 to 2 green peppers, sliced
2 4-oz. cans sliced mushrooms, drained
26-oz. jar spaghetti sauce
12 hot dog buns or sub rolls, split
2 c. shredded mozzarella cheese

Pan-fry or grill sausages until lightly browned. Add sausages, onion, peppers, mushrooms and sauce to a slow cooker. Cover and cook on low setting for 4 to 6 hours, until vegetables are tender. Serve on buns; top with cheese.

~ *Handy Tip* ~

Designate a drawer or a shelf for keeping all the little things you usually have to hunt down when expecting guests. Be sure to include matches, toothpicks, a corkscrew, coffee filters and birthday candles...you'll be glad you thought ahead!

Stephanie Norton, *Saginaw, TX*

Nana's Slow-Cooker Meatballs

I love the little bit of zip the Worcestershire sauce gives these meatballs.

Makes 4 dozen

2-1/2 c. catsup
1 c. brown sugar, packed
2 T. Worcestershire sauce
2 lbs. ground beef
1.35-oz. pkg. onion soup mix
5-oz. can evaporated milk

Combine catsup, brown sugar and Worcestershire sauce in a slow cooker; stir well and cover. Turn slow cooker to high setting and allow mixture to warm while preparing the meatballs. Combine beef, onion soup mix and evaporated milk; mix well and form into one-inch balls. Place meatballs on an ungreased 15"x10" jelly-roll pan. Bake at 325 degrees for 20 minutes; drain. Spoon meatballs into slow cooker and reduce setting to low. Cover and cook 2 to 3 hours, stirring gently after one hour.

Kelley Annis, *Massena, NY*

Cranberry Kielbasa Bites

You can use this same recipe with meatballs.

Serves 10 to 12

2 16-oz. Kielbasa sausage rings, cut into 1/2-inch pieces
2 14-oz. pkgs. mini smoked sausages
3/4 c. catsup
14-oz. can whole-berry cranberry sauce
1/2 c. grape jelly

Place all ingredients in a slow cooker; stir to mix well. Cover and cook on low setting for 7 to 8 hours.

— *Handy tip* —

Add pizzazz to an appetizer tray...glue tiny Christmas balls onto long toothpicks for serving.

Cranberry Kielbasa Bites

Tori Willis, *Champaign, IL*

Texas Two-Step Dip

My Aunt Marlene from El Paso shared this incredible dip recipe with me, and now I can't stop making it. I take it to any get-together or function I go to, and it never fails that I'm asked for the recipe.

Serves 10 to 12

1/2 lb. ground Italian pork sausage
1 onion, finely chopped
2 15-oz. cans refried beans
1-1/2 c. shredded Monterey Jack cheese
1-1/2 c. salsa
4-oz. can diced green chiles
1 t. ground cumin
corn chips or tortilla chips

Brown sausage and onion in a skillet over medium heat; drain. Spoon sausage mixture into a slow cooker. Stir in refried beans, cheese, salsa, green chiles with juice and cumin. Cover and cook on low setting, stirring occasionally, for 3 to 4 hours, until cheese is melted and dip is warmed through. Serve with chips for dipping.

Aemelia Manier, *West Branch, MI*

Hawaiian Kielbasa

You can serve this as an appetizer or over rice.

Makes 10 to 15 servings

3 lbs. Kielbasa, sliced into 2-inch chunks
15-1/4 oz. can crushed pineapple
18-oz. bottle barbecue sauce
1/2 c. brown sugar, packed
1 T. ground ginger
1 t. onion powder
1 t. garlic powder

Combine all ingredients in a slow cooker. Mix well. Cover and cook on low setting for about 2 hours, until warmed through, or on high setting for about 30 minutes.

Hawaiian Kielbasa

Easy Gumbo Meatballs

Brenda Flowers, *Olney, IL*

Easy Gumbo Meatballs

After baking, keep these warm in a slow cooker...they're a potluck favorite!

Serves 6

2 lbs. ground beef
4 slices bread, crumbled
3/4 c. evaporated milk
10-3/4 oz. can chicken gumbo soup
10-1/2 oz. can French onion soup
cooked rice
Optional: chopped fresh parsley

Combine first 3 ingredients together; form into one-inch balls. Arrange in an ungreased 13"x9" baking pan; pour soups on top. Bake, uncovered, at 350 degrees for 1-1/2 hours. Serve over cooked rice. Garnish with parsley, if desired.

Lisa Colombo, *Appleton, WI*

Oniony Crab Dip

This dip couldn't be easier to whip up...ready to go for dinner parties.

Serves 24

2 8-oz. pkgs. cream cheese, softened
3 T. butter
1 bunch green onions, chopped
1 lb. crabmeat, flaked
garlic salt to taste
onion salt to taste
crackers and garlic toast
Optional: additional chopped green onions

Combine all ingredients except crackers, toast and additional green onions in a microwave-safe bowl; microwave on high until warm. Stir well. Pour into an ungreased slow cooker; cover and keep warm on low setting. Serve with crackers and garlic toast. Garnish with additional green onions, if desired.

Chapter Two

Daily Bowls & Dishes

Soups and sides for every day of the week!
Delicious, hearty and simple soups and sides don't have to be just for company...made the slow-cooker way, they can be enjoyed any day during the week. Slow-Cooker Smoked Sausage Stew is bursting with flavor and is the perfect way to satisfy hungry tummies. Or maybe Gramps and Gran are joining you for dinner? With Cheesy Corn for a Crowd, you can toss everything into the slow cooker and focus on the family. And they'll all be asking for seconds with Cajun flare when Down-on-the-Bayou Gumbo is on the table!

Loaded Potato Soup

Tonya Sheppard, *Galveston, TX*

Loaded Potato Soup

Since this recipe takes eight hours to cook, it's best to put it on first thing in the morning so it'll be ready when you walk in the door from work.

Serves 8

4 lbs. redskin potatoes, peeled and cut into
    1/4-inch thick slices
1/2 c. onion, chopped
2 14-oz. cans chicken broth
2 t. salt
1/2 t. pepper
2 c. half-and-half
Garnish: shredded Cheddar cheese, cooked and
    crumbled bacon, sliced green onions

Layer sliced potatoes in a lightly greased 5-quart slow cooker; top with chopped onion. Stir together chicken broth, salt and pepper; pour over potatoes and onion. Broth will not completely cover potatoes and onion. Cover and cook on low setting 8 hours, or until potatoes are tender. Mash mixture with a potato masher; stir in half-and-half. Cover and cook on high setting 20 more minutes, or until mixture is thoroughly heated. Ladle into bowls and garnish.

Stephanie Carlson, *Sioux Falls, SD*

Italian Sub Cream Soup

This recipe is the result of not being able to decide which of two soup recipes to make.

The result was delicious, and it's now a family favorite!

Serves 6 to 8

1 T. olive oil
1 lb. ground Italian pork sausage
3-1/2 oz. pkg. sliced pepperoni, slices quartered
1/4 lb. deli sliced salami, slices quartered
1 green pepper, diced
1 onion, diced
2 cloves garlic, minced
2 to 3 T. all-purpose flour
28-oz. can diced tomatoes
4 c. chicken broth
salt and pepper to taste
2 t. dried oregano
1/4 t. red pepper flakes
1 c. elbow macaroni, cooked
2 c. whipping cream
1/4 c. fresh Italian parsley, chopped
Garnish: shredded mozzarella cheese, grated
    Parmesan cheese

Heat oil in a large skillet over medium heat. Brown sausage in oil; drain. Stir in pepperoni and salami; cook for one to 2 minutes. Add green pepper, onion and garlic to sausage mixture; cook for about 5 minutes, until vegetables have softened. Stir in flour. Spoon sausage mixture into a slow cooker. Add tomatoes with juice, broth and seasonings to slow cooker. Cover and cook on low setting for 3 to 4 hours, until vegetables are tender and soup has thickened. About 20 minutes before serving, stir cooked pasta, cream and parsley into soup. Garnish servings with cheeses.

Tara Horton, *Delaware, OH*

Un-Chili

My family really enjoys my chili recipe made with red beans and tomato sauce. To make it more special, the first pot of chili for the season is always served on October 1st and the last hurrah is Opening Day for the Cincinnati Reds. One September, we had a hankering for my chili, but I wasn't allowed to make it yet...so this slightly different "un-chili" recipe was created!

Serves 4 to 6

1 lb. ground beef
1 clove garlic, minced
14-1/2 oz. can black beans, drained and rinsed
1 c. beef broth
14-1/2 oz. can petite diced tomatoes
1/4 t. sugar
1 T. chili powder
1-1/2 t. cumin
salt and pepper to taste
1/4 to 1/2 c. water
1/4 c. frozen corn
Garnish: shredded Cheddar cheese, corn chips

In a skillet over medium heat, cook beef until almost browned. Add garlic and stir until beef is cooked through; drain. In a slow cooker, combine beef mixture, beans, broth, tomatoes with juice, sugar, seasonings and water. Cover and cook on high setting for 2 hours, or on low setting for 4 hours. Stir in corn for the last 15 minutes of cooking time. Garnish as desired.

Virginia Watson, *Scranton, PA*

New England Corn Chowder

Once you taste this, you'll never go back to canned chowder!

Serves 6

1/2 c. butter, melted
2 T. onion powder
2 t. dried thyme
2 stalks celery, chopped
46-oz. can clam juice
2 cubes chicken bouillon
2 bay leaves
3 16-oz. cans whole potatoes, drained and diced
3 10-oz. cans whole baby clams
2 c. light cream
2 c. milk
salt and pepper to taste

Stir together butter, onion powder, thyme and celery in a slow cooker; cover and cook on high setting for 30 minutes. Add clam juice, bouillon, bay leaves and potatoes. Cover and continue cooking on high setting for 2 hours. Add undrained clams; reduce heat to low setting. Cover and cook for 2 more hours. Stir in cream and milk; cover and cook one more hour, or until heated through. Before serving, discard bay leaves; add salt and pepper to taste.

New England Corn Chowder

Elizabeth Tipton, Knoxville, TN

Elizabeth's White Chili

*Garnish with crushed white-corn tortilla chips...
a clever use for those broken chips that linger
at the bottom of the bag!*

Serves 6 to 8

1 lb. boneless, skinless chicken breasts, cooked
    and shredded
4 15-1/2 oz. cans Great Northern beans
16-oz. jar salsa
8-oz. pkg. shredded Pepper Jack cheese
2 t. ground cumin
1/2 c. chicken broth
Optional: 12-oz. can beer or 1-1/2 c.
    chicken broth

Combine all ingredients except optional beer
or broth in a 5-quart slow cooker. Add beer or
broth for a thinner consistency, if desired. Cover
and cook on low setting for 4 hours, or until
heated through.

Kathy Murray Strunk, Mesa, AZ

Kathleen's Fabulous Chili

*This recipe is my own creation. It won first
place for 'Overall Best Chili' at a church chili
cook-off!*

Serves 6 to 8

1 lb. ground beef
1/2 to 1 lb. bacon, chopped
1 onion, chopped
1/2 green pepper, diced
2 15-1/2 oz. cans dark red kidney beans, drained
    and rinsed
15-1/2 oz. can light red kidney beans, drained
    and rinsed
15-1/2 oz. can pinto beans
16-oz. can pork & beans
15-1/2 oz. can Sloppy Joe sauce
14-1/2 oz. can diced tomatoes, drained and juice
    reserved
1/4 to 1/2 c. brown sugar, packed
salt, pepper and chili powder to taste
Garnish: sour cream, sliced green onions,
    shredded Cheddar cheese

Brown ground beef and bacon with onion and
green pepper in a skillet over medium heat; drain.
Combine all ingredients except garnish in a slow
cooker, using half of reserved tomato juice; cover
and cook on high setting until chili just begins
to simmer, about one hour. Reduce heat to low
setting; continue to simmer, covered, for 2 to
4 hours. Add remaining tomato juice if more
liquid is needed. Garnish as desired.

Kathleen's Fabulous Chili

Jill Rognrud, *McGregor, MN*

Bavarian Venison Stew

The taste of autumn in a bowl...you can use stew beef cubes instead of venison, if you'd like.

Serves 6 to 8

2 to 3-lb. venison roast, cubed
1 T. oil
15-oz. can Bavarian-style sauerkraut
5 potatoes, cubed
1 c. carrots, peeled and chopped
1 c. celery, chopped
12-oz. can beer or 1-1/2 c. apple juice
hot pepper sauce to taste

Brown venison cubes in oil on all sides in a skillet over medium heat; drain. Combine venison cubes, sauerkraut with juice and remaining ingredients in a slow cooker. Cover and cook on low setting for 8 hours.

Jennifer Stacy, *Hamler, OH*

Cheesy Corn for a Crowd

I make this yummy corn casserole every time my family gets together!

Serves 15 to 18

4 15-1/4 oz. cans corn, drained
4 15-oz. cans creamed corn
8-oz. pkg. shredded Cheddar cheese
8-oz. pkg. shredded mozzarella cheese
2 8-1/2 oz. pkgs. corn muffin mix
16-oz. container French onion dip

4 eggs, beaten

Combine all ingredients in a large bowl. Prepare a 6-quart slow cooker by either spraying with non-stick vegetable spray or putting in a disposable liner. Pour mixture into slow cooker. Cover and cook on high setting for 4-1/2 hours, or on low setting for 9 hours.

Tiffany Burdette, *Everson, WA*

Ham & Potato Soup

This satisfying soup recipe is just right! Save room for seconds, because you'll definitely want more. This soup freezes and reheats really well.

Serves 8

3-1/2 c. potatoes, peeled and diced
3-1/4 c. water
1/3 c. celery, chopped
1/3 c. onion, finely chopped
3/4 c. cooked ham, diced
6 cubes chicken bouillon
1 t. pepper
1/2 t. salt
5 T. butter
5 T. all-purpose flour
2 c. milk
Garnish: celery leaves

Combine all ingredients except butter, flour and milk in a 5-quart slow cooker. Cover and cook on low setting for 6 to 8 hours, or until potatoes are fork-tender. About 20 minutes before serving, melt butter in a saucepan over medium heat; stir in flour. Gradually add milk, stirring constantly until thickened. Stir mixture into soup in slow cooker. Cover and cook on low setting 15 to 20 more minutes, until thickened. Garnish, if desired.

Ham & Potato Soup

Chicken & Rice Soup with Mushrooms

Vickie, *Gooseberry Patch*

Chicken & Rice Soup with Mushrooms

Serves 8

1 T. olive oil
1 c. onion, chopped
1/2 c. celery, chopped
8-oz. pkg. sliced mushrooms
2 cloves garlic, minced
2 c. water
5 c. chicken broth
3 c. cooked chicken, chopped
2 T. fresh parsley, chopped
1 t. chicken bouillon granules
6-oz. pkg. long-grain and wild rice mix

Heat oil in a large skillet over medium-high heat. Add onion, celery, mushrooms and garlic. Sauté 4 minutes, or until vegetables are tender; add 2 cups water, stirring to loosen particles from bottom of skillet. Combine vegetable mixture, broth and remaining ingredients (including seasoning packet from rice mix) in a 4- or 5-quart slow cooker. Cover and cook on low setting 4 to 4-1/2 hours, until rice is tender.

Muriel Vlahakis, *Sarasota, FL*

Zucchini Parmesan

Everyone in our family loves my eggplant Parmesan. I thought I would try this alternative for one summer family gathering, because we all love Italian food. It was a big hit!

Serves 10 to 12

2 T. oil
10 zucchini, thinly sliced
garlic powder to taste
26-oz. jar spaghetti sauce
8-oz. pkg. shredded mozzarella cheese
1 to 1-1/2 c. shredded Parmesan cheese

Heat oil in a skillet over medium heat. Working in batches, sauté zucchini until tender. Layer 1/4 of zucchini in a slow cooker; sprinkle with garlic powder. Spoon 1/4 of sauce over top; sprinkle with 1/4 of cheeses. Repeat layers 3 times, ending with cheeses. Cover and cook on low setting for 2 to 4 hours, until zucchini is tender and cheese melts.

Kerry Fountain, *Ionia, MI*

Baked Beans with Sausage

This is a quick & easy hearty baked bean dish!

Serves 4 to 6

1 lb. ground pork sausage, browned and drained
48-oz. jar Great Northern beans, drained
1 c. brown sugar, packed
1 onion, chopped

Combine all ingredients in a slow cooker. Cover and cook on low setting for 4 to 6 hours.

Audrey Lett, *Newark, DE*

Slow-Cooked Hearty Pork Stew

This is a super make-ahead recipe. Freeze stew and topping in separate containers, then thaw in the fridge two days ahead of serving.

Serves 8

1-1/2 lbs. boneless pork shoulder, cubed
1 lb. Kielbasa sausage ring, sliced
14-1/2 oz. can chicken broth
2 c. onion, chopped
6 carrots, peeled and thickly sliced
2 cloves garlic, minced
2 15-oz. cans cannellini beans, drained and
   rinsed
3 T. tomato paste
1 t. dried thyme
1/2 t. pepper
14-1/2 oz. can diced tomatoes, drained
Optional: Crumb Topping

Combine all ingredients except tomatoes and Crumb Topping in a 5-quart slow cooker. Cover and cook on low setting for 8 to 10 hours, or on high setting for 4 to 5 hours. Stir in tomatoes; cover and cook an additional 10 minutes. If using Crumb Topping, place stew in a lightly greased, shallow, 3-quart casserole dish. Sprinkle with Crumb Topping; bake at 400 degrees for 15 to 20 minutes, until topping is crisp and golden.

Crumb Topping:

1-1/2 c. soft bread crumbs
1/4 c. fresh parsley, chopped
1/4 c. grated Parmesan cheese
2 T. olive oil
Toss all ingredients together.

Verona Haught, *Londonderry, NH*

Farmer's Market Stew

Autumn means the last of the farmers' markets, so gather as many fresh fall veggies as you can for this hearty dish.

Serves 6

1/2 lb. stew beef cubes
2 1/2-inch thick boneless pork chops, cubed
1 T. olive oil
2 carrots, peeled and chopped
2 parsnips, peeled and chopped
2 potatoes, peeled and chopped
1 stalk celery, chopped
2 apples, peeled, cored and cut into 1-inch cubes
2 T. quick-cooking tapioca, uncooked
1 c. apple cider
1 c. water
2 t. beef bouillon granules
Optional: 1/2 c. red wine
1/4 t. pepper
1/4 t. dried thyme
1/4 t. dried rosemary
salt to taste
Garnish: fresh rosemary, fresh thyme

Brown beef and pork in oil in a large skillet over medium heat; drain. Place vegetables and apples in a slow cooker; sprinkle with tapioca. Add beef and pork. Combine remaining ingredients except salt and garnish in a small bowl; pour over beef and pork. Cover and cook on low setting for 8 to 10 hours, or on high setting for 4 to 6 hours. Add salt to taste before serving. Garnish with rosemary and thyme.

Farmer's Market Stew

Jalapeño Chicken Chili

Lisa Case, *Clovis, CA*

Jalapeño Chicken Chili

This chili is exactly what you need for the big game! It's so easy to make, perfectly spicy, and filled with delicious ingredients for everyone!

Serves 8

2 c. chicken, cooked and cubed
4 15.8-oz. cans Great Northern beans
1 onion, chopped
1/2 c. red pepper, diced
1/2 c. green pepper, diced
2 jalapeño peppers, seeded and finely diced
2 cloves garlic, minced
1-1/2 t. ground cumin
3/4 t. salt
1/2 t. dried oregano
1/2 t. chicken bouillon granules
1/4 c. water
1 to 2 c. salsa
Optional: tortilla chips

Combine all ingredients except salsa and chips in a slow cooker. Cover and cook on low setting for 8 to 10 hours, or on high setting for 5 hours. Add salsa during last hour of cooking. Before serving, stir well to blend. Serve with tortilla chips if desired.

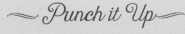

～ Punch it Up ～

Stir in a handful of greens right at the end. They wilt and become a tasty part of the soup.

Paula Lee, *Lapel, IN*

South-of-the-Border Chicken Soup

Black beans and salsa add a Mexican flair to this filling soup that's a snap to make in the slow cooker.

Serves 6 to 8

2 to 3 boneless, skinless chicken breasts
15-oz. can black beans, drained and rinsed
15-1/4 oz. can corn, drained
24-oz. jar salsa
tortilla chips
Optional: sour cream, shredded Cheddar cheese

Layer chicken, beans, corn and salsa in a slow cooker. Cover and cook on low setting for 6 to 8 hours, until juices run clear when chicken is pierced. Using 2 forks, shred chicken and return to slow cooker; ladle soup into bowls. Serve with chips and top with desired toppings.

Shelley Turner, *Boise, ID*

Sweet Potato Chili

Is there anything sweet potato doesn't taste good in? I first had this chili at a church cook-off...it won! I asked my friend for the recipe, made a few tweaks, and now it's my favorite chili ever.

Serves 6 to 8

2 sweet potatoes, peeled and cut into 2-inch chunks
1 yellow onion, diced
1 red pepper, chopped
2 cloves garlic, minced
14-1/2 oz. can diced fire-roasted tomatoes
15-oz. can kidney beans, drained and rinsed
1 T. chili powder
1 t. paprika
1/2 t. salt
1-1/2 c. water
Garnish: shredded Cheddar cheese

Combine sweet potato, onion, red pepper and garlic in a slow cooker. Stir in undrained tomatoes and remaining ingredients except garnish. Cover and cook on low setting for 6 to 8 hours, until sweet potato is tender. Using a spoon, mash a few sweet potato cubes against side of crock to thicken soup. Top servings with cheese.

Katie Cooper, *Chubbuck, ID*

Pineapple Baked Beans

This is my mother's recipe...it makes the most scrumptious baked beans.

Serves 10 to 15

28-oz. can baked beans
14-oz. bottle catsup
1-1/2 c. brown sugar, packed
15-1/4 oz. pineapple chunks, drained
1/2 lb. bacon, chopped
2 T. Worcestershire sauce
1 T. soy sauce

Add all ingredients to a slow cooker; stir well. Cover and cook on low setting for 3 to 5 hours.

Connie Bryant, *Topeka, KS*

Mamma Mia Italian Stew

This slow-cooker stew is chock-full of flavorful summer produce, with a hint of heat from hot Italian sausage.

Serves 8 to 10

1 lb. hot ground Italian sausage, browned and drained
1 eggplant, peeled and cubed
1-1/2 c. sliced green beans
2 green peppers, sliced
1 to 2 potatoes, peeled and cubed
1 large zucchini, cubed
1 large yellow squash, cubed
1 c. onion, thinly sliced
15-oz. can Italian-style tomato sauce
1/4 c. olive oil
2 t. garlic, minced
1 t. salt

Combine all ingredients in a 7-quart slow cooker; stir well. Cover and cook on low setting for 8 hours, or on high setting for 4 hours.

Mamma Mia Italian Stew

Mary Little, *Franklin, TN*

Easy Chicken Chili

Our family loves to enjoy this dish on a chilly Tennessee evening.

Serves 8 to 10

2 to 3 5-oz. cans chicken
3 15-oz. cans Great Northern beans
2 15-1/2 oz. cans hominy
16-oz. jar salsa
2 8-oz. pkgs. shredded Monterey Jack cheese

Combine all ingredients in a slow cooker, including liquid from cans. Cover and cook on low setting for 8 hours.

Susie Gray, *Winchester, IN*

Slow-Cooker Smoked Sausage Stew

Bake a pan of cornbread to serve alongside this filling stew.

Serves 4

4 to 5 potatoes, peeled and cubed
2 16-oz. cans green beans
1-lb. pkg. smoked sausage, sliced
1 onion, chopped
2 T. butter, sliced

Layer potatoes, green beans with liquid, sausage and onion in a slow cooker; dot with butter. Cook on low setting for 4 to 5 hours.

Linda Keehn, *Chatham, IL*

Bacon-Corn Chowder

Ideal for toting to a harvest bonfire supper.

Serves 4 to 6

5 c. redskin potatoes, cubed
16-oz. pkg. frozen corn
6 slices bacon, crisply cooked and crumbled
1/4 c. dried, minced onion
2 14-1/2 oz. cans chicken broth
1 c. water
2 t. garlic salt
1 t. pepper
1/4 t. turmeric
12-oz. can evaporated milk
8-oz. pkg. shredded Monterey Jack cheese
Optional: fresh chives, chopped

Combine all ingredients except milk, cheese and chives in a slow cooker. Cover and cook on low setting for 8 to 9 hours, until potatoes are tender. Stir in milk and cheese; cover and cook until cheese melts. Garnish with chives, if desired.

Bacon-Corn Chowder

Beef Stew

Claire Bertram, *Lexington, KY*

Beef Stew

This classic recipe works well in a slow cooker.

Serves 6 to 8

6 slices bacon, chopped
2 lbs. stew beef cubes
16-oz. pkg. frozen pearl onions, thawed
8-oz. pkg. mushrooms, quartered
6 redskin potatoes, quartered
2 carrots, peeled and cut into 1/2-inch pieces
14-oz. can beef broth
1 c. Burgundy, dry red wine or beef broth
2 T. tomato paste
1 T. fresh thyme leaves
1 t. salt
1/4 t. pepper
3 cloves garlic, minced
2 T. cornstarch
2 t. cold water

Cook bacon in a large skillet over medium-high heat until crisp. Remove bacon, reserving drippings in pan. Set bacon aside. Brown beef, in batches, in drippings until browned on all sides. Combine reserved bacon, beef, onions and remaining ingredients except cornstarch and water in a 5-quart slow cooker. Cover and cook on low setting for 7 hours, or until beef and vegetables are tender. Whisk together cornstarch and water. Stir into stew. Cover and cook on high setting one hour, or until slightly thickened.

Judith Jennings, *Ironwood, MI*

Turkey & Wild Rice Soup

This hearty soup is chock-full of veggies! Make it even healthier by using fat-free broth and evaporated milk, if you wish.

Serves 6

2 t. oil
1/2 c. onion, chopped
1 c. deli smoked turkey, diced
1 c. celery, diced
1 c. carrots, peeled and diced
1/2 c. long-cooking wild rice, uncooked
1 t. dried tarragon
1/4 t. pepper
2 14-1/2 oz. cans chicken broth
12-oz. can evaporated milk
1/3 c. all-purpose flour
1 c. frozen peas, thawed
Optional: 2 T. dry sherry

Heat oil in a skillet over medium heat. Add onion and cook for about 4 minutes, or until tender, stirring occasionally. Combine onion, turkey, celery, carrots, rice, tarragon and pepper in a slow cooker; stir in broth. Cover and cook on low setting for 6 to 8 hours, until vegetables and rice are tender. Mix evaporated milk and flour in a small bowl; stir into soup along with peas and sherry, if using. Cover again and cook on low setting for about 20 minutes, or until thickened.

Down-on-the-Bayou Gumbo

Sue Nealy, *Greenville, IL*

Down-on-the-Bayou Gumbo

You can't help but smile with a bowl of gumbo right in front of you! Using a slow cooker means it's ready when you get home.

Serves 6

3 T. all-purpose flour
3 T. oil
3 c. chicken broth
1/2 lb. smoked pork sausage, sliced
2 c. frozen okra
14-1/2 oz. can diced tomatoes
1 onion, chopped
1 green pepper, chopped
3 cloves garlic, minced
1/4 t. cayenne pepper
3/4 lb. cooked medium shrimp, tails removed
cooked rice
Garnish: chopped fresh parsley

Stir together flour and oil in a saucepan over medium heat. Cook, stirring constantly, for 5 minutes. Reduce heat to low; cook and stir for 10 minutes, or until mixture is reddish brown. Pour broth into a slow cooker; stir in flour mixture. Add remaining ingredients except shrimp, rice and parsley. Cover and cook on low setting for 7 to 9 hours. Add shrimp to slow cooker; mix well. Cover and cook on low setting for 30 minutes. Ladle gumbo over cooked rice in bowls. Garnish with chopped parsley.

Eleanor Paternoster, *Bridgeport, CT*

Country-Style Scalloped Potatoes

Old-fashioned flavor...fix & forget convenience!

Serves 4 to 6

6 russet potatoes, thinly sliced
1-1/2 lbs. ham steak, cubed
10-3/4 oz. can cream of mushroom soup
1-1/4 c. water
1 c. shredded Cheddar cheese
grill seasoning to taste
Optional: fresh chives, chopped

Layer potatoes and ham in a slow cooker that has been sprayed with non-stick vegetable spray. Combine remaining ingredients except garnish in a bowl; pour over potatoes and ham. Cover and cook on high setting for 3-1/2 hours, or until potatoes are fork-tender. Reduce heat to low setting; continue cooking for about one hour. Garnish with chives, if desired.

Nancy Girard, *Chesapeake, VA*

Harvest Pecan Sweet Potatoes

A delicious addition to a holiday meal...I always get lots of compliments!

Serves 8 to 10

2 29-oz. cans sweet potatoes, drained
1/3 c. plus 2 t. butter, melted and divided
2 T. sugar
1/3 c. plus 2 T. brown sugar, packed and divided
1 T. orange juice
2 eggs, beaten
1/2 c. milk
1/3 c. chopped pecans
2 T. all-purpose flour

Mash sweet potatoes in a large bowl; blend in 1/3 cup melted butter, sugar and 2 tablespoons brown sugar. Beat in orange juice, eggs and milk; spoon into a lightly greased slow cooker and set aside. Combine pecans, flour, remaining brown sugar and remaining butter in a small bowl. Spread mixture over sweet potatoes; cover and cook on high setting for 3 to 4 hours.

Barbara Cooper, *Orion, IL*

Midwestern Steakhouse Soup

If the potatoes haven't thickened the broth as much as you'd like, simply whisk 2 tablespoons cornstarch into 1/4 cup cold water and then stir into the soup and cook a little longer.

Serves 6 to 8

1-1/2 lbs. boneless beef top sirloin steak, about 1/2-inch thick, sliced into thin strips
2 T. oil
1 sweet onion, sliced
8-oz. pkg. sliced mushrooms
3 14-1/2 oz. cans beef broth
4 c. water
3 potatoes, cut into 1/2-inch cubes
2 t. Worcestershire sauce
Garnish: 8-oz. pkg. shredded Monterey Jack cheese, chopped fresh parsley

Brown steak strips in oil in a Dutch oven over medium heat for 5 minutes. Add onion and mushrooms; sauté until tender, about 5 to 10 minutes. Add remaining ingredients except garnish; simmer over low heat for 30 to 40 minutes. Transfer to a slow cooker. Cover and cook on low setting for up to 4 hours. Ladle into bowls and serve garnished with cheese and chopped parsley.

Midwestern Steakhouse Soup

Divine Seafood Chowder

Audrey Laudenat, *East Haddam, CT*

Divine Seafood Chowder

This chowder is a meal in itself. Serve with cornbread squares, slices of crusty bread and cold iced tea...don't forget the oyster crackers!

Makes 4 to 6 servings

1 onion, sliced
4 potatoes, peeled and sliced
minced garlic to taste
1 t. dill weed
2 T. butter, diced
1 c. clam juice, heated to boiling
15-oz. can creamed corn
salt and pepper to taste
1/2 lb. haddock or cod fillets
1/2 lb. medium shrimp, peeled, cleaned
  and halved
1 c. light cream, warmed

Layer all ingredients except cream in a slow cooker, placing fish and shrimp on top. Cover and cook on high setting for one hour; reduce setting to low and cook for 3 hours. Gently stir in cream just before serving.

Wendy Ramsey, *Alliance, OH*

Slow-Cooker Spanish Rice

It's hard to imagine how this tasty rice could be any easier to make!

Serves 8 to 10

2 lbs. ground beef
2 14-1/2 oz. cans petite diced tomatoes
1 onion, chopped
1 green pepper, chopped
29-oz. can tomato sauce
1 c. instant rice, uncooked

In a large skillet over medium heat, brown beef; drain. Place beef, tomatoes with juice and remaining ingredients in a slow cooker. Stir well. Cover and cook on high setting for 3 hours, or until rice is tender. Stir in a little bit of water if rice seems too dry.

Carol Lytle, *Columbus, OH*

Kielbasa Soup

This is a terric cold-weather soup...warms you right up after a hockey game!

Serves 8

1-1/2 to 2 lbs. Kielbasa sausage, thinly sliced
4 qts. water
16-oz. pkg. frozen mixed vegetables
6-oz. can tomato paste
1 onion, chopped
3 potatoes, peeled and diced
Optional: chopped fresh parsley

Combine all ingredients except parsley in a slow cooker. Cover and cook on low setting for 10 to 12 hours. Garnish individual servings with parsley, if desired.

Kathy Grashoff, *Fort Wayne, IN*

Scalloped Corn & Broccoli

Take this to your next potluck...your slow cooker will come back empty!

Serves 8 to 10

16-oz. pkg. frozen chopped broccoli
16-oz. pkg. frozen corn
10-3/4 oz. can cream of chicken soup
1 c. American cheese, shredded
1/2 c. shredded Cheddar cheese
1/4 c. milk

Combine all ingredients in a large bowl and spoon into a slow cooker. Cover and cook on low setting for 5 to 6 hours.

Daphne Mann, *Waukesha, WI*

Cheesy Crock Potatoes

A real winner...you may want to make a double batch!

Serves 4 to 6

24-oz. pkg. frozen shredded hashbrowns, thawed
10-3/4 oz. can cream of potato soup
16-oz. container ranch dip
1 to 2 c. shredded Cheddar cheese
salt, pepper and garlic powder to taste
6-oz. can French-fried onions

Combine hashbrowns, soup, dip, cheese and seasonings in a slow cooker. Cover and cook on low setting for 4 to 6 hours, stirring once. Sprinkle with onions before serving.

Kay Marone, *Des Moines, IA*

Country Chicken Stew

A savory, filling meal in a bowl.

Serves 4

4 boneless, skinless chicken thighs
3-1/2 c. chicken broth
2 c. plum tomatoes, chopped
1 c. green pepper, chopped
1 c. onion, chopped
1/2 c. long-cooking rice, uncooked
1/2 c. canned garbanzo beans, drained and rinsed
3 cloves garlic, chopped
1/2 t. salt
1/2 t. pepper
1 bay leaf
Garnish: shredded Monterey Jack cheese, diced avocado

Combine all ingredients except garnish in a slow cooker. Cover and cook on low setting for 7 to 9 hours, until chicken and rice are tender. Discard bay leaf. To serve, place a chicken thigh in each soup bowl; top with soup and garnish as desired.

Country Chicken Stew

Old-Fashioned Sage Dressing

Gina Rongved-Van Wyk, *Rapid City, SD*

Old-Fashioned Sage Dressing

How clever! Make stuffing in your slow cooker to free up the oven for other dishes like roast turkey or baked yams.

Serves 10 to 12

2 c. onion, chopped
2 c. celery, chopped
1 c. butter
2 loaves white bread, torn
1-1/2 t. dried sage
1 t. dried thyme
1/2 t. dried marjoram
1 t. poultry seasoning
1-1/2 t. salt
1/2 t. pepper
14-1/2 oz. can chicken broth
2 eggs, beaten

In a skillet, sauté onion and celery in butter until fragrant; set aside. Place bread in a large bowl; add seasonings and mix well. Add onion mixture and enough broth to moisten bread; toss. Stir in eggs and mix well. Spoon into a slow cooker. Cover and cook on low setting for 6 to 8 hours, stirring occasionally and adding more broth as needed.

Amy Thomason Hunt, *Traphill, NC*

Easy Cheesy Veggies

Who can resist double-cheesy goodness?

Serves 6 to 8

10-3/4 oz. can Cheddar cheese soup
2 t. Worcestershire sauce
20-oz. pkg. frozen new potato wedges
16-oz. pkg. baby carrots
1/4 c. celery, diced
1-1/4 c. frozen peas
1 c. shredded Cheddar cheese

In a bowl, combine soup and Worcestershire sauce; mix well and set aside. In a 4-quart slow cooker, combine all vegetables except peas; pour soup mixture over top. Cover and cook on low setting for 6 to 7 hours. Before serving, stir in peas and cheese. Cover and cook for 10 minutes longer, or until cheese is melted.

Nancy Wise, *Little Rock, AR*

Spinach Soufflé

Spice up this yummy spinach bake by substituting Mexican pepper cheese and stirring in some red pepper flakes and diced jalapeños!

Serves 8

2 10-oz. pkgs. frozen chopped spinach, thawed and drained
2 c. small-curd cottage cheese
1 c. pasteurized process cheese spread, cubed
3 eggs, beaten
2 T. butter, diced
1/4 c. all-purpose flour
1/2 t. salt

In a 3-quart slow cooker, combine all ingredients; mix well. Cover and cook on low setting for 2-1/2 hours, or until set and cheese is melted.

Staci Meyers, *Cocoa, FL*

Savory Southern-Style Greens

Be sure to save the flavorful "pot liquor," or cooking broth...use it instead of water for cooking rice.

Serves 6 to 8

2 smoked ham hocks
6 c. water, divided
3 to 4 cubes ham bouillon
2 T. sugar
2 T. vinegar brine from a jar of sliced jalapeño
    peppers
seasoned salt and pepper to taste
1 bunch collard greens, trimmed and sliced into
    1/2-inch strips
cooked rice

Combine ham hocks and 2 cups water in a stockpot; bring to a boil. Reduce heat and simmer for 15 to 30 minutes. Stir in remaining water and other ingredients except greens and rice. Transfer ham hocks and greens to a slow cooker; pour hot broth over top. Cover and cook on low setting for 8 hours or overnight, until greens are tender but not mushy, adding more water as necessary to keep slow cooker at least half full of liquid. Remove ham hocks; dice meat and return to slow cooker. For best flavor, cool and refrigerate, reheating next day at serving time. Serve over cooked rice.

Kay Marone, *Des Moines, IA*

Smashed Redskin Potatoes

Everyone loves these potatoes...a nice change from the same ol' mashed potato. They're oh-so pretty served in a big bowl, garnished with snipped chives.

Serves 10 to 12

5 lbs. redskin potatoes, quartered
1 T. garlic, minced
3 cubes chicken bouillon
8-oz. container sour cream
8-oz. pkg. cream cheese, softened
1/2 c. butter, softened
salt and pepper to taste

Place potatoes, garlic and bouillon in a large saucepan; cover with water. Bring to a boil; cook just until potatoes are tender, about 15 minutes. Drain, reserving cooking liquid. Place potatoes, sour cream and cream cheese in a large bowl; mash potatoes, adding cooking liquid as needed until desired consistency is reached. Spoon into a slow cooker; cover and cook on low setting for 2 to 3 hours. Stir in butter, salt and pepper just before serving.

Smashed Redskin Potatoes

Stephanie Edgington, *West Milton, OH*

Tasty Green Beans

*Our family loves this easy-to-make side...
it doesn't require precious oven or stovetop
space during big family gatherings!*

Serves 6 to 8

1/2 lb. bacon
4 14-1/2 oz. cans cut green beans, drained
2 14-oz. cans chicken broth
1 onion, cut into wedges
salt and pepper

In a skillet over medium heat, cook bacon until
crisp. Drain, reserving 1/2 of drippings. Crumble
bacon. Add bacon, reserved drippings and
remaining ingredients to a slow cooker; stir. Cover
and cook on low setting for 7 to 8 hours, or on high
setting for 5 hours.

Karen Hart, *Franklin, TN*

Yummy Pizza Soup

*Serve with garlic bread and a tossed green
salad for a complete meal.*

Serves 8 to 10

1 lb. ground beef
1 lb. ground Italian pork sausage
1 onion, chopped
8-oz. pkg. sliced pepperoni
28-oz. can crushed tomatoes
2 8-oz. cans tomato sauce
4-1/4 oz. can chopped black olives, drained
3 cubes chicken bouillon
2 c. water
1 t. dried oregano

1 t. dried basil
1 t. garlic powder
16-oz. pkg. medium shell pasta, uncooked
Garnish: 2 c. shredded mozzarella cheese

In a large skillet over medium heat, brown beef,
sausage and onion; drain. Add beef mixture and
remaining ingredients except pasta and cheese to
a slow cooker. Cover and cook on low setting for
4 to 6 hours. About 15 minutes before serving, cook
pasta according to package directions; drain. Serve
soup ladled over pasta in individual bowls; top
with cheese.

Jill Valentine, *Jackson, TN*

Slow-Cooker Butternut Squash Soup

*Just chop a few ingredients and combine
in the slow cooker for a delicious gourmet
soup...so easy!*

Serves 8

2-1/2 lbs. butternut squash, halved, seeded,
    peeled and cubed
2 c. leeks, chopped
2 Granny Smith apples, peeled, cored and diced
2 14-1/2 oz. cans chicken broth
1 c. water
seasoned salt and white pepper to taste
Garnish: freshly ground nutmeg, sour cream

Combine squash, leeks, apples, broth and water
in a 4-quart slow cooker. Cover and cook on high
setting for 4 hours or until squash and leeks
are tender. Carefully purée the hot soup, in 3 or
4 batches, in a food processor or blender until
smooth. Add seasoned salt and white pepper.
Garnish with nutmeg and sour cream.

Slow-Cooker Butternut Squash Soup

Grandma's Corn

Dixie Dickson, *Sachse, TX*

Grandma's Corn

An old-timey potluck favorite.

Serves 6 to 8

8-oz. pkg. cream cheese
1/4 c. butter
32-oz. pkg. frozen corn
1/3 c. sugar
Optional: 1 to 3 T. water

Let cream cheese and butter soften in slow cooker on low setting for about 10 minutes. Add corn and sugar; stir well, until corn is coated with cream cheese mixture. Cover and cook on low setting for 3 to 4 hours, stirring occasionally. If corn seems too thick, add water as needed just before serving.

Tina Butler, *Royse City, TX*

Cheesy Hashbrown Casserole

Why not let your slow cooker help prepare this popular cheesy potato casserole? I adapted this recipe as a time and space-saver for the busy holiday season.

Serves 8

32-oz. pkg. frozen shredded hashbrowns
8-oz. container sour cream
10-3/4 oz. can cream of chicken soup
1/4 c. onion, diced
1-1/2 c. shredded Cheddar cheese
1/2 c. butter, melted

salt and pepper to taste

In a large bowl, combine all ingredients. Spoon mixture into a 4-quart slow cooker that has been sprayed with non-stick vegetable spray. Cover and cook on low setting for 4 to 5 hours, until hot and bubbly throughout and crisp on the sides.

Lisa Hardwick, *Plainfield, IN*

Tea Room Broccoli-Cheese Soup

This recipe was inspired by a local tea room that I loved to visit with my family. Their soup was the best I had ever had! Sadly, the tea room closed, but my mother-in-law knew how much I loved the soup and she created this replica for me. It's really yummy, and the recipe means a lot to me because she took the time to make it just for me.

Serves 8 to 10

1/2 c. margarine
16-oz. pkg. frozen broccoli cuts
2 10-3/4 oz. cans cream of chicken soup
2 10-3/4 oz. cans cream of mushroom soup
4 c. milk
16-oz. pkg. pasteurized process cheese spread, cubed

In a skillet over medium heat, melt margarine. Add broccoli; cook and stir for 5 to 10 minutes. Add broccoli mixture to a slow cooker; stir in remaining ingredients. Cover and cook on low setting, stirring occasionally, for 3 to 4 hours.

Joanne Callahan, *Far Hills, NJ*

Mexican Roast Pork Stew

I like experimenting with low-fat recipes, and this one is a real crowd-pleaser! Served over brown rice, it makes an excellent and nutritious one-dish meal.

Serves 10 to 12

4 to 6-lb. pork picnic roast, cut into bite-size
    pieces
1/4 c. chili powder
2 T. ground cumin
1 T. coriander
1 sweet onion, chopped
2 cloves garlic, pressed
1 T. oil
2 28-oz. cans stewed tomatoes
15-oz. can black beans, drained and rinsed
2 dried poblano peppers, finely chopped and
    seeds removed
2 c. apple juice or water
cooked brown rice

Toss pork with seasonings. In a skillet over medium heat, sauté pork, onion and garlic in oil until browned on all sides. To a large slow cooker, add pork mixture, tomatoes with juice, beans, peppers and juice or water. Cover and cook on low setting for 9 hours. Serve ladled over rice.

Erin Ho, *Renton, WA*

Erin's Ham & Cheese Soup

It was a dark stormy evening driving home from work. I wanted something comforting and cozy for dinner and I thought, "Why haven't I ever made ham and cheese soup?" The wheels started turning, and I created this. The recipe has been shared among family & friends. Everyone who's tried it has been very satisfied!

Serves 8 to 10

1 red pepper, diced
1 white onion, diced
3 to 4 cloves garlic, minced
1 jalapeño pepper, finely chopped and seeds
    removed
3/4 lb. cooked ham, diced
2 10-3/4 oz. cans Cheddar cheese soup
2 10-3/4 oz. cans cream of potato soup
3 c. pasteurized process cheese spread, diced
8-oz. pkg. shredded Cheddar Jack cheese
4 c. milk
1 c. whipping cream
1 t. salt, or to taste
2 t. pepper
1 T. garlic herb seasoning

Combine all ingredients in a slow cooker; mix well. Cover and cook on low setting for 4 to 6 hours, or on high setting for 2 to 3 hours, until bubbly and cheese is melted.

Erin's Ham & Cheese Soup

Donna's Green Chile Stew

Donna Wilson, *Chesapeake, VA*

Donna's Green Chile Stew

My husband grew up in New Mexico. Being a military family, we've since moved all over the place. I created this recipe for him so he could enjoy all the favorite flavors of his home state. It's a regular at our dinner table.

Serves 8

1 to 2-lb. boneless pork roast, cubed
1 onion, diced
1 T. oil
2 15-1/2 oz. cans white hominy, drained
28-oz. can green chile enchilada sauce
4-oz. can diced green chiles
2 to 3 cloves garlic, minced
2 potatoes, peeled and diced
2 carrots, peeled and thinly sliced
salt and pepper to taste
flour tortillas

In a skillet over medium heat, brown pork and onion in oil. Transfer to a large slow cooker; add remaining ingredients except tortillas. Mix well. Cover and cook on low setting for 6 to 8 hours. To serve, scoop mixture onto tortillas.

Krista Marshall, *Fort Wayne, IN*

Split Pea Soup

Even though I do 99 percent of the cooking in our house, it's nice to know that if for some reason I couldn't, our family wouldn't starve because my husband is a pretty amazing cook. He has a few recipes that are his "signature" dishes, and this is one of them.

Serves 8 to 10

2 12-oz. pkgs. dry split peas
1 lb. carrots, peeled and finely diced
1 onion, finely diced
1 lb. cooked ham, diced
salt and pepper to taste

Add all ingredients to a slow cooker; add enough water to cover. Cover and cook on high setting for 6 to 8 hours, stirring occasionally, until peas cook down and soup becomes very thick. Add additional water to reach desired consistency, if needed.

~ *Punch it Up* ~

A great way to get the tastebuds happy. Try whisking in some soft, roasted garlic.

Vickie, *Gooseberry Patch*

Garlicky Ham & Lima Soup

There's a down-home goodness to lima beans and ham that I can never get enough of. This hearty soup is perfect to take to potlucks and get-togethers...sure to warm everyone up!

Serves 8

1 lb. dried lima beans
1 onion, peeled and diced
8 cloves garlic, peeled
28-oz. can diced tomatoes
3-1/2 c. water
2 c. cooked ham, diced
2 t. paprika
salt to taste
Garnish: grated Parmesan cheese

Place beans in a bowl and cover with water. Let soak overnight; drain. Combine beans, onion and garlic in a slow cooker. Stir in tomatoes and 3-1/2 cups water. Add ham, paprika and salt; stir. Cover and cook on low setting for 8 hours, or until beans are tender. Transfer one to 2 cups of soup into a blender and process until smooth; stir back into soup in slow cooker to thicken. Garnish servings with Parmesan cheese.

Karen Swartz, *Woodville, OH*

Hearty Meatball Stew

Busy day ahead? Prepare the ingredients for this easy recipe the night before. For a special treat, serve it ladled into individual sourdough bread bowls.

Serves 8

1 lb. new potatoes, cubed
16-oz. pkg. baby carrots
1 onion, sliced
2 4-oz. cans sliced mushrooms, drained
16-oz. pkg. frozen meatballs
12-oz. jar beef gravy
14-1/2 oz. can Italian-seasoned diced tomatoes
3-1/4 c. water
pepper to taste
14-1/2 oz. can corn, drained

In a large slow cooker, layer all ingredients except corn in the order listed. Cover and cook on low setting for 8 to 10 hours. About one hour before serving, stir in corn.

Hearty Meatball Stew

German Potato Salad

Maureen Laskovich, *Allison Park, PA*

German Potato Salad

I was looking for something new for Easter dinner when I ran across this recipe. I tried it and my family loved it!

Serves 4

4 c. potatoes, peeled and cubed
6 slices bacon, crisply cooked, crumbled and
  2 T. drippings reserved
3/4 c. onion, chopped
10-3/4 oz. can cream of chicken soup
1/4 c. water
2 T. cider vinegar
1/2 t. sugar
pepper and dried parsley to taste
Garnish: fresh parsley, chopped

Cover potatoes with water in a saucepan; simmer over medium heat about 15 minutes, or just until tender. Drain and let cool. Sauté onion in reserved drippings over medium-high heat until tender, about 5 minutes. Blend together soup, water, vinegar, sugar and pepper in a large bowl; add bacon and onion. Add potatoes and parsley; mix well and pour into a slow cooker. Cover and cook on low setting for 4 hours. Serve warm or at room temperature. Garnish with fresh parsley.

Christina Mendoza, *Alamogordo, NM*

Chris's Chuckwagon Beans

I combined three or four of my favorite recipes to create this one. We always serve these meaty beans with a side of hot cornbread.

Serves 6 to 8

1 lb. dried navy or pinto beans, rinsed
1 lb. ground beef
1 onion, chopped
1 clove garlic, minced
1 green pepper, chopped
6 c. water
salt to taste
1/2 t. dried oregano
1/4 t. cayenne pepper, or to taste
8-oz. can tomato sauce

Add beans to a large kettle; cover with water. Bring to boiling; boil, covered, for 2 minutes. Remove from heat and let stand for one hour. Drain. Add beans to a large slow cooker. In a skillet, brown beef with onion, garlic and green pepper. Drain. Add beef mixture to beans in slow cooker; stir in 6 cups water and remaining ingredients. Add more water, if necessary, so that bean mixture is covered. Cover and cook on low setting for 10 hours, or on high setting for 6 hours, until beans are tender.

Nancy Dynes, *Goose Creek, SC*

Lillian's Beef Stew

My mother made this for us when we were small children, and now I make it for my own family. It's a wonderful dinner to come home to on a cold day.

Serves 8

2 lbs. stew beef cubes
2 potatoes, peeled and quartered
3 stalks celery, diced
4 carrots, peeled and cut into thick slices
2 onions, quartered
2 c. cocktail vegetable juice
1/3 c. quick-cooking tapioca, uncooked
1 T. sugar
1 T. salt
1/2 t. dried basil
1/4 t. pepper

Arrange beef and vegetables in a 4-quart slow cooker. Combine remaining ingredients in a bowl; pour into slow cooker. Cover and cook on low setting for 8 to 10 hours.

Barbara Ferree, *New Freedom, PA*

Creamy Crab & Shrimp Bisque

This is one of the easiest and tastiest cream soup recipes I have ever tried. It always brings rave reviews, and people cannot believe how simple it is to put together in the slow cooker!

Serves 6 to 8

1 lb. cooked crabmeat, chopped
1/2 lb. cooked shrimp, chopped
10-3/4 oz. can cream of celery soup
10-3/4 oz. can cream of potato soup
10-3/4 oz. can cream of asparagus soup
2 c. half-and-half
2 c. milk
1/4 c. butter
seafood seasoning to taste

Combine all ingredients in a large slow cooker. Cover and cook on low setting for 3 to 4 hours.

Beth Schlieper, *Lakewood, CO*

Red Beans & Rice

My friend Sharon made this yummy dish for our family about eight years ago, and I've made it ever since. Tastes great served with a side of coleslaw!

Serves 8 to 10

16-oz. Kielbasa sausage ring, sliced into bite-size pieces
4 to 5 15-oz. cans red beans, drained
2 14-1/2 oz. cans diced tomatoes
1 onion, chopped
hot pepper sauce to taste
salt, pepper and red pepper flakes to taste
cooked white rice

Place all ingredients except rice in a slow cooker. Mix well. Cover and cook on low setting for 8 hours. Serve ladled over rice.

Red Beans & Rice

Lisa's Chicken Tortilla Soup

Lisa Johnson, *Hallsville, TX*

Lisa's Chicken Tortilla Soup

South-of-the-border flavor coming right up!

Serves 6 to 8

4 14-1/2 oz. cans chicken broth
4 10-oz. cans diced tomatoes with green chiles
1 c. canned or frozen corn
30-oz. can refried beans
5 c. cooked chicken, shredded
Garnish: shredded Mexican-blend cheese, corn
   chips or tortilla strips, chopped fresh cilantro

Combine all ingredients except garnish in a
slow cooker. Cover and cook on low setting for
4 to 5 hours. Garnish bowls of soup as desired.

~ Change it Up ~

Plain yogurt works much like sour cream
when added to soups. It will give a tangy flavor
to any soup.

Patty Flak, *Erie, PA*

Ham & Lentil Stew

Comfort food that's good for you too!

Serves 8

1 c. cooked ham, diced
2 c. dried lentils
2 c. carrots, peeled and diced
2 c. celery, diced
1 c. onion, chopped
1 T. garlic, minced
4 c. water
1 t. dried oregano
2-1/4 c. chicken broth
1/4 t. pepper
6-oz. pkg. fresh baby spinach
1 T. lemon juice

Combine all ingredients except spinach and
lemon juice in a slow cooker. Cover and cook on
low setting for 7 to 8 hours, until lentils are tender.
Stir in spinach; cover and cook for 5 minutes. Stir
in lemon juice just before serving.

Kimberly Ascroft, *Merritt Island, FL*

Hearty Carrot Soup

When left with a late-season garden full of carrots, I make carrot soup! It's a great way to use 'em up...everybody loves it.

Serves 6

32-oz. container sodium-free beef broth
2-1/2 lbs. carrots, peeled and sliced
1/4 c. onion, diced
2 cloves garlic, minced
2 T. brown sugar, packed
1 T. ground ginger
1/4 c. whipping cream

In a slow cooker, combine broth, carrots, onion and garlic. Cover and cook on high setting for 5 hours, or on low setting for 8 hours, until carrots break apart easily. Working in batches, transfer contents of slow cooker to a blender or food processor, or use an immersion blender. Blend soup for about one minute, until desired consistency is reached. Stir in remaining ingredients. Serve warm.

Kathie Poritz, *Burlington, WI*

Snowy Day Chili

Here in Wisconsin, snow is inevitable, but shoveling sidewalks isn't so dreaded when there's a pot of chili simmering on the stove!

Serves 8 to 10

2 lbs. ground beef or venison
2 c. onion, chopped
4 c. tomato sauce
4 c. water
15-oz. can kidney beans, drained and rinsed
6-oz. can tomato paste
1/4 c. Worcestershire sauce
2 T. brown sugar, packed
1 T. seasoned salt
1 T. lemon juice
3 bay leaves
chili powder to taste
Optional: hot pepper sauce to taste
Garnish: shredded Cheddar cheese, chopped
    onion, sour cream, corn chips

Brown meat in a large stockpot over medium heat; drain. Stir in remaining ingredients except garnish. Transfer to a slow cooker. Cover and cook for 3 to 4 hours, stirring occasionally. Discard bay leaves. Garnish as desired.

Snowy Day Chili

Ultimate White Chicken Chili

Sonda Huhta, *Loveland, CO*

Ultimate White Chicken Chili

I often make this recipe for the annual harvest party at my daughter's elementary school. It's enjoyed by teachers, parents and children alike!

Serves 8

2 14-1/2 oz. cans chicken broth
4 c. chicken, cooked and chopped
2 4-oz. cans chopped green chiles
3 15-oz. cans Great Northern beans, drained and rinsed
2 c. shredded Monterey Jack cheese
1/8 t. cayenne pepper
1 t. dried oregano
2-1/2 t. ground cumin
16-oz. container sour cream

Add all ingredients except sour cream to a slow cooker. Cover and cook on low setting for 6 to 8 hours. Shortly before serving, stir in sour cream; heat through.

— *Change it Up* —
Add flour, cornstarch or other thickener... starches thicken soup and give it body.

Susan Ahlstrand, *Post Falls, ID*

Slow-Cooker Taco Soup

A friend from my Bible study group made her version of this and everyone loved it! I changed a few ingredients to suit my tastes.

Serves 8 to 10

1 lb. ground beef
1 onion, diced
1 clove garlic, minced
12-oz. bottle green taco sauce
4-oz. can green chiles, chopped
2 to 3 15-oz. cans black beans, drained and rinsed
15-1/4 oz. can corn, drained
15-oz. can tomato sauce
2 c. water
1-1/4 oz. pkg. taco seasoning mix
Garnish: sour cream, shredded Cheddar cheese, corn chips

Brown beef, onion and garlic in a large skillet over medium heat; drain. In a slow cooker, combine beef mixture and remaining ingredients except garnish. Cover and cook on high setting one hour. Serve with sour cream, shredded cheese and corn chips, if desired.

Laura Witham, *Anchorage, AK*

Vegetarian Mexican Chili

I sampled this chili while visiting a friend of mine, and I loved it so much I asked for the recipe! I make it whenever I need an easy meal to feed a crowd.

Serves 6 to 8

2 15-oz. cans ranch-style beans
2 10-oz. cans diced tomatoes with green chiles
15-1/2 oz. can white hominy, drained
15-1/2 oz. can golden hominy, drained
1-oz. pkg. ranch salad dressing mix
3 c. vegetable broth
Garnish: shredded Cheddar cheese, crushed
    tortilla chips

In a slow cooker, combine beans with liquid, tomatoes with juice and remaining ingredients except garnish. Cover and cook on low setting for 8 hours, or on high setting for 6 hours. Garnish as desired.

Paula Forman, *Lancaster, PA*

Creamy Mac & Cheese

My daughter, now grown, always signed me up to make my slow-cooker macaroni for Girl Scouts, 4-H and many school events. She always came home with an empty crock! For an easy meal, just stir in some cooked shrimp or Kielbasa sausage.

Serves 6 to 8

16-oz. pkg. elbow macaroni, uncooked
1/4 c. margarine, sliced
2 c. milk
1 t. salt
8-oz. pkg. pasteurized process cheese spread,
    cubed
1 c. shredded Cheddar cheese

Cook macaroni according to package directions, until just barely tender; drain. Add macaroni and remaining ingredients to a slow cooker. Cover and cook on low setting for one hour, stirring occasionally.

Creamy Mac & Cheese

Sweet Potato Casserole

Bethi Hendrickson, *Danville, PA*

Sweet Potato Casserole

This yummy dish is a must for any fall brunch!

Serves 8

6 c. sweet potatoes, cooked and mashed
1/3 c. butter, melted
2 T. sugar
3 T. brown sugar, packed
1 T. orange juice
2 eggs, beaten
1/2 c. fat-free half-and-half or milk
2 t. cinnamon
1 t. nutmeg

In a large bowl, blend potatoes, butter and sugars. Stir in remaining ingredients. Transfer mixture to a lightly greased slow cooker, spreading evenly. Spoon Pecan Topping evenly over top, pressing down lightly. Cover and cook on high setting for 3 to 4 hours.

Pecan Topping:

1/3 c. chopped pecans, toasted
1/3 c. brown sugar, packed
2 T. all-purpose flour
2 T. butter, melted

In a bowl, combine all ingredients.

Penny Sherman, *Ava, MO*

Asian-Inspired Short Rib Soup

A new Asian restaurant opened up in town, and I tried a dish very similar to this one. I love the slightly spicy flavor of this soup. This is my effort to recreate it at home...a pretty good interpretation, I'd say!

Serves 6 to 8

6 lbs. beef short ribs, cut into serving-size
    pieces
4 c. low-sodium chicken broth
1/3 c. soy sauce
1/4 c. sugar
3 T. fresh ginger, peeled and grated
2 T. sriracha hot chili sauce
2 T. toasted sesame oil
4 cloves garlic, finely chopped
1 bunch green onions
12-oz. pkg. rice noodles, uncooked
Garnish: grated carrot, sliced cucumber,
    chopped fresh cilantro, lime wedges

Place ribs in a large slow cooker; set aside. In a bowl, whisk together broth, soy sauce, sugar, ginger, chili sauce, oil and garlic. Thinly slice white part of onions and stir into broth mixture. Spoon broth mixture over ribs. Cover and cook on high setting for 6 hours, until ribs are very tender. About 30 minutes before serving, prepare noodles according to package directions. Drain; divide noodles evenly among 6 bowls. Skim fat from soup in slow cooker; ladle broth and ribs over noodles. Garnish servings as desired.

Janet Powell McKee, *Manteca, CA*

Old-Fashioned Oxtail Soup

If it's cold and blustery outside, you will be warm and satisfied with our Grandma Nance's soup. It's a tradition for Thanksgiving and Christmas eves at our house.

Serves 8 to 10

2 lbs. beef oxtails, cut into serving-size pieces
1/2 c. onion, chopped
2 to 3 T. oil
1/2 c. red wine or beef broth
1/2 head cabbage, chopped
28-oz. can crushed tomatoes
4 c. tomato juice
4 c. water
2 T. salt
1 c. chopped vegetables, such as carrots, celery, onion and green beans
16-oz. pkg. frozen corn
16-oz. pkg. wide egg noodles, uncooked

In a skillet over medium heat, brown oxtails with onion in oil. Cook and stir until onion is tender. Pour in wine or broth. Increase heat to high; cook and stir, scraping browned bits from the skillet, until liquid is boiling. Carefully transfer contents of skillet to slow cooker. Add remaining ingredients except noodles. Cover and cook on low setting for 8 to 9 hours, stirring occasionally. About 15 minutes before serving, prepare noodles according to package directions; drain. Stir into soup.

Patricia Skalka, *Medford, NJ*

Spicy Spinach-Sausage Soup

I created this recipe one night, and it was a hit with my family. I serve it to friends too, and they all love it...serve with slices of crusty bread for soaking up all the tasty broth!

Serves 8

1-1/2 lbs. ground hot Italian pork sausage
48-oz. can stewed tomatoes
49-oz. can chicken broth
8-oz. pkg. sliced mushrooms
16-oz. pkg. baby carrots, sliced
10-oz. pkg. frozen chopped spinach, thawed
1 onion, chopped
1 t. garlic pepper
1/4 c. grated Parmesan cheese

Brown sausage in a skillet over medium heat; drain. Combine cooked sausage, undrained tomatoes and remaining ingredients in a slow cooker; mix well. Cover and cook on low setting for 8 to 9 hours.

Spicy Spinach-Sausage Soup

Chapter Three

Worry-Free
Dinners

Making Dinnertime Doable! Having dinner on the table and ready to eat can really be a simple feat! Your slow cooker is ready to help you out with delicious home-cooked meals that will make 'em shout with glee. You'll find amazing recipes bursting with flavor like super-juicy Feta Greek Chicken and Slow-Cooker Roast for Tacos. This chapter also has all the comforts of home cooking like Penn Dutch Ham Potpie, Chicken Cordon Bleu and mouthwatering Mexican Hamburgers.

Lisanne Miller, *York, ME*

Irish Corned Beef Dinner

Serve with rye bread and spicy mustard for a tasty meal.

Serves 6

3-lb. corned beef brisket
4 to 6 potatoes, peeled and quartered
1 lb. carrots, peeled, halved and cut into sticks
1 head cabbage, cut into wedges
2 onions, quartered
12-oz. can regular or non-alcoholic beer
1 bay leaf
2 to 3 c. water

Place corned beef in a 6-quart slow cooker. Arrange vegetables around beef; add beer, bay leaf and enough water to cover. Cover and cook on high setting for 3-1/2 to 4 hours. Discard bay leaf. To serve, arrange vegetables on a large serving platter. Slice corned beef and arrange on platter.

Tami Hoffman, *Litchfield, NH*

Slow-Cooker Creamy Apricot Chicken

Serve with creamy mashed potatoes and your favorite veggie. Then pour on spoonfuls of the creamy apricot sauce.

Serves 4 to 6

8-oz. bottle Russian salad dressing
12-oz. jar apricot preserves
1 to 2 lbs. boneless, skinless chicken breasts

Combine salad dressing and preserves together; set aside. Arrange chicken in a 5-quart slow cooker; pour dressing mixture on top. Cover and cook on high setting for one hour, then on low setting for 3 hours, or until done.

Sharon Beach, *Potosi, MO*

Shredded Beef Sandwiches

I love to toast the split buns in the oven for a few minutes before serving.

Serves 10 to 12

12-oz. jar sliced pepperoncini
4-lb. beef chuck roast
1-3/4 t. dried basil
1-1/2 t. dried oregano
1-1/2 t. garlic powder
1-1/4 t. salt
1/4 t. pepper
1/4 c. water
1 onion, sliced
10 to 12 sandwich buns, split and toasted

Pour pepperoncini with liquid into a 5-quart slow cooker; add roast. Mix together spices, salt and pepper in a small bowl; sprinkle over roast. Add water and onion. Cover and cook on low setting for 8 to 9 hours, until meat is tender. Remove roast; shred using 2 forks. Return meat to slow cooker; mix well. Using a slotted spoon, place meat on buns.

Shredded Beef Sandwiches

Kris Couveau, *Soldotna, AK*

Family-Favorite Swiss Steak

I've been making this tender steak in yummy tomato gravy for more than 30 years. It's so delicious served with fluffy mashed potatoes!

Serves 5 to 6

1 c. all-purpose flour
salt and pepper to taste
2 lbs. beef round steak, cut into serving-size
   pieces
2 T. oil
1 onion, diced
1 c. celery, diced
1 green pepper, diced
10-1/2 oz. can tomato soup
1/4 c. water
1 T. cornstarch
mashed potatoes

In a large plastic zipping bag, combine flour, salt and pepper. Add steak pieces, turning and pressing to coat well in flour mixture. In a skillet over medium-high heat, heat oil; brown steaks on both sides, but do not cook through. To a slow cooker, add onion, celery, green pepper and soup. Whisk together water and cornstarch; pour over top. Add steak pieces. Cover and cook on high setting for 6 to 8 hours, or on low setting for 10 to 12 hours. Stir before serving. Serve steak over mashed potatoes; top with tomato gravy from slow cooker.

Dana Thompson, *Prospect, OH*

Slow-Cooker Roast for Tacos

Don't forget to offer all the tasty taco toppers...shredded cheese, sour cream, lettuce, tomatoes, onions and salsa. Olé!

Makes 10 cups

4 to 5-lb. beef chuck roast
1 T. chili powder
1 t. ground cumin
1 t. onion powder
1 t. garlic powder
2 14-1/2 oz. cans Mexican-style stewed
   tomatoes
taco shells

Place roast in a 5 to 6-quart slow cooker; sprinkle with seasonings. Pour tomatoes with juice over roast. Cover and cook on low setting for 8 to 10 hours. Using 2 forks, shred roast and spoon into taco shells.

Slow-Cooker Roast for Tacos

Linda Sinclair, *Valencia, CA*

Swedish Cabbage Rolls

Comfort food...just like Mom used to make.

Serves 6

12 large leaves cabbage
1 egg, beaten
1/4 c. milk
1/4 c. onion, finely chopped
1 t. salt
1/4 t. pepper
1/2 lb. ground beef
1/2 lb. ground pork
1 c. cooked rice
8-oz. can tomato sauce
1 T. brown sugar, packed
1 T. lemon juice
1 t. Worcestershire sauce
Garnish: sour cream

Immerse cabbage leaves in a large saucepan of boiling water for about 3 minutes, until limp; drain well and set aside. Combine egg, milk, onion, salt, pepper, beef, pork and cooked rice in a bowl; mix well. Place about 1/4 cup meat mixture in the center of each cabbage leaf; fold in sides and roll ends over meat. Arrange cabbage rolls in a slow cooker. Combine remaining ingredients except garnish in a small bowl and pour over rolls. Cover and cook on low setting for 7 to 9 hours. Spoon sauce over rolls and garnish with sour cream.

Regina Vining, *Warwick, RI*

Spaghetti for a Crowd

After cooking for several hours, this spaghetti's flavor is tremendous! There's no added oil, so this sauce is low-fat too.

Serves 6 to 10

5 29-oz. cans tomato sauce
3 6-oz. cans tomato paste
1 onion, chopped
3 cloves garlic, minced
3 T. dried rosemary
3 T. dried oregano
3 T. dried thyme
3 T. dried parsley
1/8 t. red pepper flakes
1 bay leaf
8 to 10 c. cooked spaghetti
Garnish: shaved Parmesan cheese, fresh thyme sprigs

Combine all ingredients except spaghetti and garnish in a 6-quart slow cooker. Cover and cook on high setting for 3 to 4 hours, stirring frequently. Discard bay leaf. Serve over cooked spaghetti; sprinkle with Parmesan cheese and thyme sprigs.

Spaghetti for a Crowd

Sweet & Spicy Baby Back Ribs

Ann Speil, *San Antonio, TX*

Sweet & Spicy Baby Back Ribs

Ribs done right are a home run!

Makes 8 servings

2 slabs baby back ribs (about 5 lbs.), halved
3 green onions, chopped
1 T. fresh ginger, minced
1-1/2 t. garlic, minced
1 T. oil
12-oz. bottle chili sauce
8-oz. bottle hoisin sauce
1/2 c. applesauce
1/2 c. regular or non-alcoholic beer
2 T. Worcestershire sauce
1 T. country-style Dijon mustard
1 to 3 t. hot pepper sauce

Preheat broiler with oven rack 5-1/2 inches from heat. Coat the rack of a broiler pan and broiler pan with non-stick vegetable spray. Place ribs on rack in broiler pan. Broil 10 minutes. Meanwhile, sauté green onions, ginger and garlic in hot oil in a small saucepan over medium heat for 3 to 5 minutes, until tender. Stir in remaining ingredients. Bring to a boil; reduce heat to medium-low and simmer 5 minutes. Arrange half of ribs in a single layer in a lightly greased 7-quart oval slow cooker. Pour half of sauce mixture over ribs. Top with remaining ribs in a single layer. Pour remaining sauce mixture over ribs. Cover and cook on low setting 4 hours, or until tender.

Beth Bennett, *Stratham, NH*

Feta Greek Chicken

I didn't know what to make for dinner, but I had some chicken in the freezer and I love Greek seasoning...so this is what I came up with. It turned out surprisingly good!

Serves 8 to 10

8 to 10 boneless, skinless chicken breasts
2 T. Greek seasoning
1 c. water
1-1/2 c. crumbled feta cheese
2 14-1/2 oz. cans diced tomatoes with basil, garlic and oregano

Place chicken in a slow cooker; sprinkle with seasoning. In a bowl, combine water, cheese and tomatoes with juice. Pour over chicken. Cover and cook on high setting for 3 to 4 hours, until chicken is no longer pink.

~ *Take it to Go* ~

Be sure to have take-out containers on hand to send guests home with leftovers...if there are any!

Ann Christie, *Glasgow, KY*

Mexican Hamburgers

This wonderful stick-to-your-ribs sandwich cooks in the slow cooker, so it's always ready when we come in from the cold. A really tasty meal, yet extremely easy.

Serves 8 to 10

2 lbs. ground beef
2-1/4 c. water, divided
28-oz. can tomato purée
1 t. chili powder
pepper to taste
8 to 10 hamburger buns, split

Brown beef with one cup water in a skillet over medium heat; drain. Spoon beef into a slow cooker. Stir in remaining water and other ingredients except buns. Cover and cook on low setting for 4-1/2 to 5 hours, stirring occasionally, until heated through. Spoon beef mixture onto buns.

Roberta Oest, *Astoria, IL*

Steamburgers

My family & friends love this simple sandwich recipe. It's a perfect old-fashioned favorite paired with a chocolate cola or a root beer float!

Serves 8 to 10

2 lbs. ground beef chuck
2-1/4 T. onion soup mix

1 T. Worcestershire sauce
1/4 t. pepper
1/2 c. water
8 to 10 hamburger buns, split
Optional: catsup

Brown beef in a skillet over medium heat; drain. Spoon beef into a slow cooker; stir in soup mix, sauce, pepper and water. Cover and cook on low setting for 2 to 4 hours, until heated through and liquid is absorbed. Spoon onto buns for sandwiches; top with catsup, if desired.

Marilyn Morel. *Keene, NH*

Easy Southern-Style Pork Barbecue

This Southern slow-cooker favorite is also known as pulled-pork barbecue.

Serves 6 to 8

3 to 4-lb. pork roast
1/4 c. water
2 T. smoke-flavored cooking sauce
pepper to taste
6 to 8 sandwich buns, split
Optional: favorite barbecue sauce, coleslaw

Place pork roast in a 4 to 5-quart slow cooker. Add water; sprinkle evenly with cooking sauce and pepper to taste. Cover and cook on high setting for one hour and then on low setting for 6 to 8 hours. Remove roast from slow cooker; shred meat with a fork. Place meat on buns; top with barbecue sauce and a scoop of coleslaw, if desired.

Easy Southern-Style Pork Barbecue

Fajita Rice Bowls

Marcie Loveless, *Savannah, GA*

Fajita Rice Bowls

My husband loves Tex Mex-inspired food, but he's a very picky eater. I devised this recipe by combining a couple of recipes that featured his favorite things. It's perfect for a crisp fall evening.

Serves 2 to 4

1 lb. ground beef
salt and pepper to taste
1 onion, chopped
1 green pepper, chopped
1/4 to 1/2 c. chipotle-lime marinade
16-oz. can crushed tomatoes
8-oz. can tomato sauce
1 c. beef broth
cooked rice
Garnish: sour cream, shredded cheese, tortilla
   chips

In a skillet over medium heat, brown beef with salt and pepper; drain. Place beef in a slow cooker. In the same skillet, sauté onion and green pepper in marinade for 5 minutes, or until tender. Add to slow cooker; pour in tomatoes with juice, tomato sauce and broth. Season with more salt and pepper, if desired. Cover and cook on low setting for 2 to 4 hours, until heated through. Serve over rice; top with sour cream, cheese and tortilla chips, if desired.

Laura Harp, *Bolivar, MO*

Beef Enchiladas

Cheesy and easy! Serve with tortilla chips.

Serves 6 to 8

1 lb. ground beef, browned and drained
15-1/2 oz. can pinto beans, drained and rinsed
15-oz. can corn, drained
10-3/4 oz. can cream of mushroom soup
10-3/4 oz. can nacho cheese soup
10-oz. can enchilada sauce
1/2 c. onion, chopped
1/2 c. sliced black olives
4 corn tortillas
2 c. shredded Cheddar cheese, divided
Optional: shredded lettuce, chopped tomato

Combine all ingredients except tortillas, shredded cheese, lettuce and tomato in a large bowl. Place one tortilla in the bottom of a slow cooker; spoon one-fourth of the beef mixture over tortilla, followed by 1/2 cup cheese. Repeat layers until all ingredients are used, ending with cheese. Cover and cook on high setting for one hour, or until cheese is melted and bubbling. Top with lettuce and tomato, if desired.

Lenore Mincher, *Patchogue, NY*

German Sauerbraten

Serve with spaetzle noodles tossed with butter and topped with chopped parsley.

Serves 12 to 14

4 to 5-lb. beef rump roast
2 t. salt
1 t. ground ginger
2-1/2 c. water
2 c. cider vinegar
2 onions, sliced
1/3 c. sugar
2 T. pickling spice
1 t. whole peppercorns
8 whole cloves
2 bay leaves
2 T. oil
16 to 20 gingersnaps, crushed

Rub roast all over with salt and ginger; place in a deep glass bowl and set aside. Combine water, vinegar, onions, sugar and spices in a saucepan; bring to a boil. Pour over roast; turn to coat. Cover roast and refrigerate for 3 days, turning twice each day. Remove roast, reserving marinade; pat dry. Heat oil in a Dutch oven; brown roast on all sides. Place roast in a slow cooker. Strain marinade, reserving half of onions and spices. Pour 1-1/2 cups marinade, onions and spices over roast; refrigerate remaining marinade. Cover and cook on low setting for 6 to 7 hours, until roast is tender. Remove roast to a platter; keep warm. Discard onions and spices; add enough of refrigerated marinade to liquid from slow cooker to equal 3-1/2 cups. Pour into a saucepan; bring to a boil. Add crushed gingersnaps; simmer until gravy thickens. Slice roast; serve with gravy.

Rowena Sjovall, *Lithia, FL*

Papaya-Tomato Chicken

A very simple and flavorful slow-cooker recipe using papaya jelly and zesty canned tomatoes.

Serves 4

4 chicken leg quarters
salt and pepper to taste
1 c. papaya jelly
10-oz. can diced tomatoes with green chiles

Pat chicken dry; sprinkle with salt and pepper. Place in a slow cooker. In a bowl, combine jelly and tomatoes with juice. Pour over chicken. Cover and cook on low setting for 6 hours.

Joan Brochu, *Hardwick, VT*

Braciola Stuffed Beef

If you've never tried this, you don't know what you're missing!

Serves 6

2 lbs. boneless beef round steak
1/2 c. seasoned dry bread crumbs
1/2 c. grated Parmesan cheese
1 T. garlic, minced
1 egg, beaten
1/4 t. pepper
2 eggs, hard-boiled, peeled and minced
32-oz. jar meatless spaghetti sauce, divided
hot cooked linguine pasta

Place steak between 2 lengths of wax paper; pound until thin and set aside. Mix together bread crumbs, cheese, garlic, egg, pepper and minced eggs in a bowl; spread over steak. Roll up steak and tie at one-inch intervals with kitchen string. Spread one cup spaghetti sauce in the bottom of a slow cooker; set a rack on top. Place rolled-up steak on rack; cover with remaining sauce. Cover and cook on low setting for 6 to 8 hours, until steak is very tender. Slice between strings and serve over hot linguine.

Braciola Stuffed Beef

Julie Pak, *Henryetta, OK*

Smoky Hobo Dinner

Away from home all day? This slow-cooker creation will have dinner waiting for you!

Serves 6

5 potatoes, peeled and quartered
1 head cabbage, coarsely chopped
16-oz. pkg. baby carrots
1 onion, thickly sliced
salt and pepper to taste
14-oz. pkg. smoked pork sausage, sliced into
   2-inch pieces
1/2 c. water

Spray a slow cooker with non-stick vegetable spray. Layer vegetables, sprinkling each layer with salt and pepper. Place sausage on top. Pour water down one side of slow cooker. Cover and cook on low setting for 6 to 8 hours.

Sharon Tillman. *Hampton, VA*

Carolina Chicken Pitas

My family just loves this with its zesty pepper flavor.

Serves 4

1 onion, chopped
1 lb. boneless, skinless chicken thighs
1 t. lemon-pepper seasoning
1/2 t. dried oregano
1/2 c. plain yogurt
4 rounds pita bread, halved and split

Combine all ingredients except yogurt and pita bread in a slow cooker; mix well. Cover and cook on low setting for 6 to 8 hours. Just before serving, remove chicken from slow cooker and shred with 2 forks. Return shredded chicken to slow cooker; stir in yogurt. Spoon into pita bread.

Sherry Toil, *Boston, MA*

Lemon-Rosemary Chicken

Rather than removing the slow-cooker lid to check on the chicken, it's best to gently tap the lid to release the condensation so you can see inside.

Serves 4

4-lb. chicken
1 lemon, halved
3 sprigs fresh rosemary
2 cloves garlic, peeled
3 T. butter, divided
salt and pepper to taste
Garnish: lemon wedges, fresh rosemary sprigs

Rinse chicken and pat dry. Place lemon halves, 3 rosemary sprigs, garlic and 2 tablespoons butter inside cavity of chicken. Fold wing tips under chicken; tie legs together with kitchen string. Sprinkle chicken with salt and pepper. Place chicken, breast-side up, on a small rack inside an oval slow cooker. Cover and cook on high setting for 4 to 4-1/2 hours, until an instant-read meat thermometer inserted into thigh registers 165 degrees. Melt remaining one tablespoon butter in a small bowl. Transfer chicken, breast-side up, to an aluminum foil-lined baking sheet. Brush chicken with melted butter; broil for 2 to 3 minutes to brown skin. Let stand 10 minutes on a cutting board before carving and serving. Garnish with lemon wedges and rosemary sprigs.

Lemon-Rosemary Chicken

Pineapple Chicken

Tonya Lewis, *Crothersville, IN*

Pineapple Chicken

Very simple...very good!

Serves 6

6 boneless, skinless chicken breasts
salt, pepper and paprika to taste
20-oz. can pineapple tidbits, drained
2 T. Dijon mustard

Arrange chicken in a slow cooker; sprinkle with salt, pepper and paprika. Set aside. Mix together pineapple and mustard in a bowl; spread over chicken. Cover and cook on high setting for 3 to 4 hours.

Cynthia Stimson, *Lake City, FL*

Chicken & Cornbread

You can add a drained can of green beans to the stuffing mix for a real all-in-one meal!

Serves 4

4 boneless, skinless chicken breasts
10-3/4 oz. can cream of mushroom soup
6-oz. pkg. cornbread stuffing mix
1/2 c. water

Place chicken in a slow cooker and set aside. Mix together remaining ingredients in a bowl; pour over chicken. Cover and cook on low setting for 6 to 8 hours.

Robin Hill, *Rochester, NY*

Wednesday Salmon Loaf

Weeknights are busy for our family, so I depend on my slow cooker to help keep us out of the drive-thru lane! This easy recipe is one of our favorites. Just add a steamed veggie or tossed salad.

Serves 6

2 15-oz. cans salmon, drained
14-1/2 oz. can diced tomatoes
4 c. dry bread crumbs
1 green pepper, chopped
1 t. lemon juice
10-3/4 oz. can cream of onion soup
4 eggs, beaten
1 t. garlic powder
1 t. Greek seasoning
2 chicken bouillon cubes, crushed
10-3/4 oz. can cream of celery soup
1/4 to 1/2 c. milk

In a bowl, combine salmon, tomatoes with juice and remaining ingredients except cream of celery soup and milk. Mix well. Pour into a slow cooker that has been sprayed with non-stick vegetable spray. Cover and cook on low setting for 4 to 6 hours. Before serving, combine cream of celery soup and milk in a saucepan; cook and stir over medium heat until heated through. Spoon over individual servings.

Hope Davenport, *Portland, TX*

Slow-Cooker Ham & Broccoli Meal-in-One

This main dish rice casserole cooks up while you are away...a truly trouble-free meal!

Serves 6 to 8

1 c. long-cooking rice, cooked
16-oz. jar pasteurized process cheese sauce
2 10-3/4 oz. cans cream of chicken soup
2 16-oz. pkgs. frozen chopped broccoli, thawed
salt and pepper to taste
1 lb. cooked ham cubes

Combine all ingredients in a slow cooker except ham. Cover and cook on low setting for 3-1/2 hours. Add ham, and mix well. Cover and cook for an additional 15 to 30 minutes.

Melanie Lowe, *Dover, DE*

Brown Sugar Ham

With only a few ingredients, you can create the most amazing flavor for this boneless ham.

Serves 15 to 20

1/2 c. brown sugar, packed
1 t. dry mustard
1 t. prepared horseradish
1/4 c. cola, divided
5 to 6-lb. boneless smoked ham, halved

Combine brown sugar, mustard, horseradish and 2 tablespoons cola in a bowl; mix well. Rub over ham; place in a slow cooker. Drizzle remaining cola over ham. Cover and cook on low setting for 8 to 10 hours, until a meat thermometer inserted in thickest part of ham reads 140 degrees.

Roberta Goll, *Chesterfield, MI*

Shredded Pork Sandwiches

Pass the coleslaw...perfect with these tender pork sandwiches!

Serves 40

8-lb. pork shoulder roast
1-oz. pkg. onion soup mix
1 c. barbecue sauce
12-oz. can beer or 1-1/2 c. beef broth
40 sandwich buns, split
Garnish: extra barbecue sauce

Combine all ingredients except buns and extra sauce in a 6-quart slow cooker. Cover and cook on low setting for 8 hours. Remove roast from cooking liquid and refrigerate liquid. Using 2 forks, shred roast. Skim fat from surface of cooled liquid. Stir cooking liquid to taste into shredded meat; mix well. Spoon into buns; serve extra sauce on the side.

Shredded Pork Sandwiches

The Best Pot Roast Ever

Joan Brochu, Hardwick, VT

The Best Pot Roast Ever

This roast cooks up so tender...you'll love the gravy too.

Serves 6 to 8

2 c. water
5 to 6-lb. beef pot roast
1-oz. pkg. ranch salad dressing mix
0.7-oz. pkg. Italian salad dressing mix
0.87-oz. pkg. brown gravy mix
6 to 8 potatoes, peeled and cut into 1-inch pieces
8 to 10 carrots, peeled and sliced

Pour water into a 7-quart slow cooker; add roast. Combine mixes in a small bowl; sprinkle over roast. Cover and cook on low setting for 6 to 7 hours; add potatoes and carrots during the last 2 hours of cooking.

Pauletta Dove, Williamson, WV

Lemon-Lime Ham

Use your choice of a boneless or semi-boneless ham.

Serves 10

6-lb. cooked ham
20-oz. bottle lemon-lime soda

Place ham in a 5 to 6-quart slow cooker; pour soda over top. Cover and cook on low setting for 8 to 10 hours. Slice to serve.

Jen Licon-Conner, Gooseberry Patch

Veggie-Stuffed Burritos

It's easy to get the kids to eat their veggies when you serve these healthy veggie burritos with all the trimmings!

Serves 8 to 10

2 T. chili powder
2 t. dried oregano
1-1/2 t. ground cumin
1 sweet or russet potato, peeled and diced
15-oz. can black beans or pinto beans, drained and rinsed
4 cloves garlic, minced
1 onion, halved and thinly sliced
1 jalapeño pepper, seeded and chopped
1 green pepper, chopped
1 c. corn
3 T. lime juice
1 T. fresh cilantro, chopped
8-oz. pkg. shredded Cheddar Jack cheese
8 to 10 flour tortillas
Garnish: sour cream

Combine spices in a small bowl; set aside. In a slow cooker, layer potato, beans, half of spice mixture, garlic, onion, peppers, remaining spice mixture and corn. Cover and cook on low setting for 5 hours, or until potato is tender. Stir in lime juice and cilantro. To assemble burritos, spoon some cheese into the center of each tortilla. Top with one cup of veggie mixture from the slow cooker. Wrap and place burritos seam-side down on an ungreased baking sheet. Cover with aluminum foil; bake at 350 degrees for 20 minutes. Serve topped with sour cream.

Elisha Wiggins, *Suwanee, GA*

Barbecue Chicken

Barbecue cooking at its very best. Share with your friends any night of the week!

Serves 4

4 boneless, skinless chicken breasts
1 c. barbecue sauce
3/4 c. chicken broth
1 sweet onion, sliced
salt and pepper to taste

Place all ingredients in a slow cooker; stir gently. Cover and cook on low setting for 6 to 7 hours, or on high setting for 3 hours.

Debbie Byrne. *Clinton, CT*

Autumn Supper Chicken

With just a few ingredients, this is ready for the slow cooker in no time...go jump in the fall leaves!

Serves 4

4 boneless, skinless chicken breasts
1-1/4 oz. pkg. taco seasoning mix
1 c. salsa
1/4 c. sour cream
tortillas or cooked rice

Place chicken breasts in a lightly greased slow cooker; sprinkle seasoning mix over chicken. Top with salsa; cover and cook on low setting for 8 hours. Remove chicken to a plate; shred and set aside. Add sour cream to salsa mixture; stir in chicken. Serve with tortillas or over cooked rice.

Diana Chaney, *Olathe, KS*

Sesame Chicken

All the flavor of traditional sesame chicken is in this recipe, but without the work of breading and frying the chicken pieces.

Serves 4 to 6

1-1/4 c. chicken broth
1/2 c. brown sugar, packed
1/4 c. cornstarch
2 T. rice vinegar
2 T. soy sauce
2 T. sweet chili sauce
2 T. honey
2 t. sesame oil
1-1/2 lbs. boneless, skinless chicken breasts, cut into 1-inch pieces
2 c. sugar snap peas
2 c. carrots, peeled and crinkle-cut
1-1/2 T. sesame seed, toasted
hot cooked rice
Garnish: chopped green onions

Whisk together fi rst 8 ingredients in a 4-quart slow cooker. Stir in chicken. Cover and cook on high setting 2-1/2 hours, or until chicken is no longer pink, stirring after 1-1/2 hours. Steam sugar snap peas and carrots until crisp-tender. Stir vegetables and sesame seeds into the slow cooker. Serve over cooked rice. Garnish with green onions.

Sesame Chicken

Glazed Corned Beef

Claire Bertram, *Lexington, KY*

Glazed Corned Beef

This brisket simmers all day in the slow cooker until fork-tender. Baste it before you serve...so simple!

Serves 4

4 to 5-lb. corned beef brisket
2-1/2 T. mustard
2 t. prepared horseradish
2 T. red wine vinegar
1/4 c. honey

In a 5-quart slow cooker, cover brisket with water. Cover and cook on low setting for 10 to 12 hours, or until tender. Place corned beef in an ungreased 13"x9" baking pan. In a small bowl, combine mustard, horseradish, vinegar and honey; baste beef. Bake, uncovered, at 400 degrees for 20 minutes, or until brisket browns; baste occasionally.

Jo Ann, *Gooseberry Patch*

Tried & True Meatloaf

Thanks to the slow cooker, this recipe is so easy to make!

Serves 4 to 6

1-1/2 lbs. ground beef
3/4 c. bread crumbs
2 eggs, beaten
3/4 c. milk
1 onion, chopped
1 t. salt

1/4 t. pepper
1/4 c. catsup
2 T. brown sugar, packed
1 t. dry mustard
1/4 t. nutmeg

Combine beef, bread crumbs, eggs, milk, onion, salt and pepper in a bowl; form mixture into a loaf. Place in a 3-quart oval slow cooker; cover and cook on high setting one hour. Reduce heat to low setting and cook 4 to 5 hours. Whisk together remaining ingredients; pour over beef. Cover and cook on high setting 15 more minutes.

Teri Eklund, *Olympia, WA*

Savory Turkey Loaf

My famous alternative to traditional meatloaf!

Serves 8

2 lbs. ground turkey
3/4 c. dry bread crumbs
1/2 c. applesauce
1 t. poultry seasoning
2 cloves garlic, minced
1/4 c. onion, minced
1 egg, lightly beaten
salt and pepper to taste
1/4 t. paprika

In a large bowl, combine all ingredients except paprika. Mix well. Form into a loaf or a round shape; place in a slow cooker. Sprinkle with paprika. Cover and cook on low setting for 5 to 6 hours.

Marge Dicton, *Bartonsville, PA*

Easy Special Pot Roast

Serves 6

10-3/4 oz. can Cheddar cheese soup
10-3/4 oz. can golden mushroom soup
10-3/4 oz. can French onion soup
3-lb. beef chuck roast

Mix soups in a slow cooker; top with roast. Cover and cook on low setting for 8 to 9 hours, turning roast halfway through cooking time if possible.

Kendall Hale, *Lynn, MA*

Hot Turkey & Stuffing Sandwiches

All the comforting flavors of Thanksgiving in a warm, satisfying sandwich! This is a great way to use up leftover turkey too.

Makes 12 servings

2 to 3 boneless, skinless turkey thighs, cubed
1 onion, chopped
1 stalk celery, chopped
1 carrot, peeled and chopped
14-oz. pkg. stuffing mix
2 c. chicken broth
12 sandwich buns, split

Add all ingredients except buns to a 3-1/2 to 4-quart slow cooker; stir well. Cover and cook on low setting for 8 to 9 hours. To serve, scoop about 1/2 cup turkey mixture onto each bun.

Deborah She eld, *Huntsville, TX*

Carne Guisada

Serve this hearty Mexican stew with warm tortillas, guacamole and shredded cheese...also great with cornbread and greens!

Serves 6

2 lbs. beef rump roast, trimmed and cubed
salt and pepper to taste
2 lbs. potatoes, peeled and chopped
10-3/4 oz. can cream of mushroom with roasted garlic soup
4-oz. can chopped green chiles
1 t. ground cumin

Sprinkle beef cubes with salt and pepper. Combine with remaining ingredients in a slow cooker. Cover and cook on low setting for 8 to 10 hours. If desired, mash lightly with a potato masher after cooking.

Carne Guisada

Chinese-Style Barbecue Pork

Ruth Leonard, *Columbus, OH*

Chinese-Style Barbecue Pork

I like to serve this dish with chopsticks just for fun.

Serves 6

2-lb. boneless pork roast
1/4 c. soy sauce
1/4 c. hoisin sauce
3 T. catsup
3 T. honey
2 t. garlic, minced
2 t. fresh ginger, peeled and grated
1 t. dark sesame oil
1/2 t. Chinese 5-spice powder
1/2 c. chicken broth
cooked rice
Garnish: chopped green onion

Place roast in a large plastic zipping bag and set aside. Whisk together remaining ingredients except broth, rice and garnish; pour over roast. Seal bag; refrigerate at least 2 hours, turning occasionally. Place roast in a slow cooker; pour marinade from bag over roast. Cover and cook on low setting for 8 hours. Remove pork from slow cooker; keep warm. Add broth to liquid in slow cooker; cover and cook on low setting for 30 minutes, or until thickened. Shred pork with 2 forks and stir into sauce in slow cooker. Serve over cooked rice; garnish with chopped green onions.

Jennifer Vander Meersh, *Rock Island, IL*

Creamy Chicken Casserole

This casserole is a winner!

Serves 4 to 6

32-oz. pkg. onion-flavored frozen potato puffs
4 to 6 boneless, skinless chicken breasts
10-3/4 oz. can cream of mushroom soup

Place potato puffs in a 4- or 5-quart slow cooker. Place chicken breasts on top; pour soup over all. Cover and cook on high setting for 4 to 6 hours, or on low setting for 8 to 10 hours.

Beth Goblirsch, *Minneapolis, MN*

3-Meat Slow-Cooker Chili

This chili is very hearty and perfect for cold days.

Makes about 13 cups

1 lb. ground beef, browned and drained
1 lb. ground sausage, browned and drained
1 lb. bacon, crisply cooked and crumbled
4 15-oz. cans tomato sauce
3 16-oz. cans kidney beans, drained and rinsed
2 T. chili seasoning
15-1/4 oz. can corn, drained

Place beef, sausage and bacon in a greased 6-quart slow cooker; stir intomato sauce, beans and seasoning. Cover and cook on low setting 4 to 6 hours; add corn during last hour.

Kimberly Adams, *Tacoma, WA*

Chicken Pot Pie

Scoop into individual bowls and top with one or two flaky biscuits warm from the oven.

Serves 6

32-oz. container chicken broth
2 10-3/4 oz. cans cream of chicken soup
2 c. milk
3 boneless, skinless chicken breasts, cooked
    and cubed
2 c. frozen peas and carrots
1 t. salt
1-1/2 t. pepper
1-1/2 t. curry powder

Put all ingredients in a 6-quart slow cooker; stir to blend. Cover and cook on low setting for 6 to 7 hours, until hot and bubbly.

Sally Kohler, *Webster, NY*

Sally's Supreme Corned Beef

Use a little cornstarch to thicken the broth after removing the brisket from the slow cooker...it makes really good gravy for the noodles.

Serves 4 to 6

2 to 3-lb. corned beef brisket
12-oz. bottle chili sauce
1.35-oz. pkg. onion soup mix

12-oz. can cola
cooked egg noodles

Place brisket in a slow cooker. Mix remaining ingredients except noodles in a bowl; pour over brisket. Cover and cook on low setting for 6 to 8 hours. Slice beef and serve over noodles.

Ashley Whitehead, *Sidney, TX*

Easy Slow-Cooker Steak

Like lots of gravy? Use two envelopes of soup mix and two cans of soup.

Makes 5 servings

2 to 2-1/2 lb. beef round steak
1-1/2 oz. pkg. onion soup mix
10-3/4 oz. can cream of mushroom soup

Slice steak into 5 serving-size pieces; place in a slow cooker. Add soup mix, 1/4 cup water and soup. Cover and cook on low setting for 6 to 8 hours.

Easy Slow-Cooker Steak

Creamy Chicken & Asparagus

Ellen Lockhart, *Blacksburg, VA*

Creamy Chicken & Asparagus

Serves 4

4 boneless, skinless chicken breasts
10-3/4 oz. can cream of chicken soup
2 c. milk
pepper to taste
dried, minced onion to taste
2 to 4 slices pasteurized process cheese
   spread, diced
1 lb. fresh asparagus, trimmed and cut into
   1-inch pieces
3 to 4 c. cooked rice

Arrange chicken in a 4-quart slow cooker. Combine soup, milk, pepper, onion and cheese in a bowl; pour over chicken. Cover and cook on low setting for 7 hours. Add frozen asparagus; increase heat to high setting. Cover and cook for one hour, or until asparagus is crisp-tender. Serve over cooked rice.

Patricia Wissler, *Harrisburg, PA*

Sweet-and-Sour Chicken

This yummy meal travels well. I often take it to new moms and recovering shut-ins.

Serves 6

2 lbs. boneless, skinless chicken breasts or
   thighs, cubed
2 12-oz. jars sweet-and-sour sauce
16-oz. pkg. frozen stir-fry vegetable
   blend, thawed
cooked rice

Combine chicken and sauce in a slow cooker. Cover and cook on low setting for 8 to 10 hours, until chicken is tender. About 10 minutes before serving, stir in vegetables. Cover and cook on high setting for 10 minutes, or until vegetables are crisp-tender. Serve over rice.

Brenda Smith, *Monroe, IN*

Hot Chicken Slow-Cooker Sandwiches

Sandwiches in the slow cooker...what could be easier?

Makes 24 sandwiches

28-oz. can cooked chicken, undrained
2 10-3/4 oz. cans cream of chicken soup
4 T. grated Parmesan cheese
7 slices bread, toasted and cubed
24 dinner rolls

In a large bowl, combine all ingredients, except dinner rolls, and pour into a 5-quart slow cooker. Cover and cook on low setting for 3 hours. Serve on rolls.

Teri Lindquist, *Gurnee, IL*

French Country Chicken

This recipe is completely my own, and we really love it. It has a very fancy taste but takes only minutes to prepare. The wine in this recipe really makes this dish, but broth can be substituted.

Serves 6

1 onion, chopped

6 carrots, peeled and sliced diagonally

6 stalks celery, sliced diagonally

6 boneless, skinless chicken breasts

1 t. dried tarragon

1 t. dried thyme pepper to taste

10-3/4 oz. can cream of chicken soup

1-1/2 oz. pkg. onion soup mix

1/3 c. dry white wine or chicken broth

2 T. cornstarch

cooked rice

Combine onion, carrots and celery in the bottom of a slow cooker. Arrange chicken on top; sprinkle with seasonings. Combine chicken soup and onion soup mix in a bowl; spoon over chicken. Cover and cook on high setting for 4 hours, stirring after one hour. At serving time, stir together wine or broth and cornstarch in a small bowl; pour over chicken and mix well. Cook, uncovered, for 10 more minutes, or until thickened. Stir again; serve over rice.

Ellie Brandel, *Milwaukie, OR*

Sweet-and-Sour Beef

This easy recipe is delicious on a cold day. Serve on its own, or over rice or pasta.

Serves 6 to 8

2 lbs. stew beef cubes

2 T. oil

2 c. carrots, peeled and thickly sliced

2 onions, chopped

1 green pepper, chopped

20-oz. can pineapple chunks, drained and juice reserved

15-oz. can tomato sauce

1/2 c. vinegar

1/2 c. light molasses

1/4 c. sugar

2 t. chili powder

2 t. paprika

1 t. salt

Optional: 1/4 c. cornstarch

In a large skillet over medium heat, brown beef in oil; drain. Combine beef, carrots, onions, pepper and pineapple in a large slow cooker. Stir well. In the same skillet, combine remaining ingredients except cornstarch; cook and stir over medium heat until well blended and heated through. Pour over beef mixture in slow cooker, stirring to coat. Cover and cook on high setting for 4 hours, or on low setting for 6 to 7 hours. For a thicker sauce, about 15 minutes before serving, dissolve cornstarch in reserved pineapple juice. Stir into slow cooker; cook for 15 minutes longer, or until thickened.

Sweet-and-Sour Beef

Tangy Teriyaki Sandwiches

Kelly Alderson, *Erie, PA*

Tangy Teriyaki Sandwiches

What a combination of flavors...what a winner!

Serves 4

1-1/2 lbs. skinless turkey thighs
1/2 c. teriyaki baste and glaze sauce
3 T. orange marmalade
1/4 t. pepper
4 hoagie buns, split
Garnish: sliced green onions

Combine all ingredients except buns and garnish in a slow cooker; cover and cook on low setting for 9 to 10 hours. Remove turkey from slow cooker and shred meat, discarding bones; return to slow cooker. Increase heat to high setting. Cover and cook for 10 to 15 minutes, until sauce is thickened. Serve on hoagie buns. Garnish with green onions.

Margie Kirkman, *High Point, NC*

Tummy-Pleasing Pizza Pasta

I tossed this together because I wanted something a little different...and something that wouldn't heat up the house!

Serves 6

1-1/2 lbs. ground beef
1 onion, chopped
16-oz. pkg. rigatoni pasta, cooked
4 c. shredded mozzarella cheese

2 14-oz. cans pizza sauce
Optional: 1 c. sliced mushrooms
8-oz. pkg. sliced pepperoni

In a skillet over medium heat, brown beef with onion; drain. In a slow cooker, alternate layers of beef mixture, pasta, cheese, sauce, mushrooms, if using, and pepperoni. Cover and cook on low setting for 4 to 5 hours.

Carol Patterson, *Deltona, FL*

Honey-Chipotle Pulled Pork

This slow-cooker pulled pork is easy and delicious. Chipotle peppers in adobo sauce combined with honey create a delicious sweet-heat combination that is guaranteed to be a hit!

Serves 8 to 10

3 lbs. boneless pork chops or pork roast
1 c. catsup
3/4 c. honey
2 canned chipotle peppers in adobo sauce, chopped

Place pork in a lightly greased slow cooker. Cover and cook on low setting for 8 hours. Drain liquid and remove fat, if needed. Shred pork with 2 forks. In a bowl, combine catsup, honey and chipotle peppers; pour over pork. Stir to combine; warm through.

Stacie Avner, *Delaware, OH*

Tex-Mex Chili Dogs

Plain ol' chili dogs are a thing of the past at our house!

Serves 10

1-lb. pkg. hot dogs
2 15-oz. cans chili without beans
10-3/4 oz. can Cheddar cheese soup
4-oz. can chopped green chiles
10 hot dog buns, split
Garnish: chopped onions, crushed corn chips,
    shredded Cheddar cheese

Place hot dogs in a slow cooker. Combine chili, soup and green chiles in a large bowl; pour over hot dogs. Cover and cook on low setting for 4 to 5 hours. Serve hot dogs in buns; top with chili mixture and garnish as desired.

Vickie, *Gooseberry Patch*

Summer Vegetable Fettuccine

Try this meatless pasta dish and discover a new favorite way to use up your summertime abundance of zucchini and yellow squash.

Serves 6

2 T. butter
1 zucchini, sliced
1 yellow squash, sliced
2 carrots, peeled and thinly sliced
1-1/2 c. sliced mushrooms
1 lb. broccoli, chopped
4 green onions, sliced
2 to 3 cloves garlic, minced
1/2 t. dried basil
1/4 t. salt
1/2 t. pepper
1 c. grated Parmesan cheese
12-oz. pkg. fettuccine pasta, uncooked
1 c. shredded mozzarella cheese
1 c. whipping cream
2 egg yolks, beaten

Use butter to grease the inside of a slow cooker. Place vegetables, seasonings and Parmesan cheese in slow cooker. Cover and cook on high setting for 2 hours, or until vegetables are tender. Cook pasta according to package directions; drain. Add pasta, mozzarella cheese, cream and egg yolks to slow cooker. Stir to blend well. Cover and cook on high setting for 30 minutes longer, or until heated through.

Summer Vegetable Fettuccine

Heather McClintock, *Columbus, OH*

Savory Pot Roast

For a thicker gravy, combine one tablespoon cornstarch and 2 tablespoons water. Add to gravy in slow cooker once roast is removed. Cook, uncovered, for 15 minutes, or until desired thickness.

Serves 6 to 8

3 to 4-lb. beef chuck roast
1/2 t. meat tenderizer
pepper to taste
1 t. olive oil
10-3/4 oz. can cream of mushroom soup
1-1/2 oz. pkg. onion soup mix
1/2 c. merlot wine or beef broth

Sprinkle roast on all sides with tenderizer and pepper. Brown roast in hot oil in a large skillet over medium heat. Transfer to a slow cooker. Combine soup, soup mix and wine or broth; pour over roast. Cover and cook on low setting for 6 to 8 hours. Remove roast to a serving platter; keep warm.

～ Punch it Up ～

Save delicate herbs like parsley, cilantro, tarragon, chives, and basil for the last minute, or they will lose their fresh flavor and bright color.

Jackie Smulski, *Lyons, IL*

Classic Chicken Cacciatore

Also try this rich, saucy stew served over rice or thin spaghetti.

Serves 3 to 4

2 T. olive oil
2 boneless, skinless chicken breasts, cut into strips
1/2 c. all-purpose flour
pepper to taste
1/2 c. chicken broth, divided
1 onion, chopped
1 green pepper, chopped
2 cloves garlic, minced
2 T. fresh Italian parsley, chopped
1/2 t. dried oregano
1/2 t. dried basil
14-oz. can diced Italian tomatoes
14-oz. jar Italian pasta sauce with vegetables
8-oz. pkg. mushrooms, chopped
6-oz. pkg. penne pasta, cooked
Garnish: grated Parmesan cheese

Heat oil in a skillet over medium heat. Coat chicken in flour and sprinkle with pepper; brown in skillet 3 to 5 minutes on each side. Place chicken in a 5-quart slow cooker on high setting. Stir in 1/4 cup broth. Add onion, green pepper, garlic and herbs; cover and cook until onion is tender. Add tomatoes, pasta sauce, mushrooms and remaining 1/4 cup broth; cover and cook to a slow boil, about 30 minutes to one hour. Serve over cooked pasta; sprinkle with Parmesan cheese.

Classic Chicken Cacciatore

Greek Chicken Pitas

Peggy Pelfrey, *Fort Riley, KS*

Greek Chicken Pitas

Top with crumbled feta cheese and sliced black olives.

Serves 4

1 onion, diced
3 cloves garlic, minced
1 lb. boneless, skinless chicken breasts, cut into strips
1 t. lemon-pepper seasoning
1/2 t. dried oregano
1/4 t. allspice
1/4 c. plain yogurt
1/4 c. sour cream
1/2 c. cucumber, peeled and diced
4 rounds pita bread, halved and split

Place onion and garlic in a 3- to 4-quart slow cooker; set aside. Sprinkle chicken with seasonings; place in slow cooker. Cover and cook on high setting for 4 to 5 hours, until chicken is no longer pink. Stir together yogurt, sour cream and cucumber in a small bowl; chill. Fill pita halves with chicken and drizzle with yogurt sauce.

Lisa Ludwig, *Fort Wayne, IN*

Swiss Steak

Your family will love this flavorful version of an old favorite. Pick up a container of heat & eat mashed potatoes for an easy side.

Serves 4

2-lb. beef chuck roast, cut into serving-size pieces
3/4 c. all-purpose flour, divided
2 to 3 T. oil
14-1/2 oz. can diced tomatoes
1 onion, sliced
1 red pepper, sliced
1 stalk celery, chopped
1 T. browning and seasoning sauce
mashed potatoes or cooked rice

Coat beef with 1/2 cup flour; sauté in oil in a skillet over medium heat until browned on all sides. Arrange beef in a 5-quart slow cooker. Combine tomatoes with juice, onion, pepper, celery and sauce in a bowl; pour over beef. Cover and cook on low setting for 6 to 8 hours. Slowly stir in remaining 1/4 cup flour to make gravy, adding a little water if necessary. Cover and cook on high setting for 15 minutes, or until thickened. Serve over mashed potatoes or hot cooked rice.

Nancy Stizza-Ortega, *Oklahoma City, OK*

Italian Sausage & Penne

Pop some garlic bread in the oven...dinner is ready!

Serves 4

3/4 lb. hot Italian sausage links, cut into
   bite-size pieces
1 red pepper, chopped
1/2 onion, chopped
26-oz. jar spaghetti sauce
8-oz. pkg. penne pasta, cooked

Stir together all ingredients except pasta in a slow cooker. Cover and cook on low setting for 7 to 8 hours. At serving time, stir in cooked pasta.

Wendy Lee Paffenroth, *Pine Island, NY*

Divine Chicken

Create this recipe with the foods on hand, and the family will love it!

Serves 6

6 boneless, skinless chicken breasts
2 10-3/4 oz. cans cream of chicken soup
1-1/4 c. milk
3 c. frozen carrots
1-1/2 c. frozen broccoli flowerets
1-1/2 oz. pkg. onion soup mix
3 to 4 c. cooked rice or pasta

Combine all ingredients except rice or pasta in a 4-quart slow cooker. Cover and cook on low setting for 6 to 8 hours. Using a slotted spoon, arrange chicken and vegetables on cooked rice or pasta. Top with sauce from slow cooker.

Jennifer Inacio, *Hummelstown, PA*

Jen's Pulled Pork

There's no right or wrong amount of sauce to use...simply stir in as much as you'd like. You can also add sliced jalapeños, minced garlic or sautéed onions and green peppers.

Serves 8 to 10

3 to 4-lb. boneless pork loin roast, halved
2-ltr. bottle cola
2 28-oz. bottles honey barbecue sauce
8 to 10 hamburger buns, split

Place roast in a 5-quart slow cooker; add cola. Cover and cook on high setting one hour; reduce heat to low setting and cook, fat-side up, 10 to 12 more hours. Remove from slow cooker; remove and discard any fat. Discard cooking liquids; clean and wipe slow cooker with a paper towel. Shred pork and return to slow cooker; add barbecue sauce to taste. Cover and cook on low setting one more hour, or until heated through. Add more sauce, if desired. Serve on buns.

Jen's Pulled Pork

Kristi Duis, *Maple Plain, NY*

Fiesta Chicken Pronto

Super juicy chicken bursting with flavor.

Serves 8

8 boneless, skinless chicken breasts
16-oz. can black beans, drained and rinsed
10-3/4 oz. can cream of chicken soup
2 T. taco seasoning mix
1/4 c. salsa

Arrange chicken in a slow cooker. Combine remaining ingredients in a bowl and pour over chicken. Cover and cook on high setting for 3 hours.

Tracy McIntire, *Delaware, OH*

Cheddar Cheese Strata

Makes a delightful brunch dish.

Serves 4 to 6

8 slices bread, crusts trimmed
8-oz. pkg. shredded sharp Cheddar cheese
4 eggs
1 c. light cream
1 c. evaporated milk
1 T. dried parsley
1/4 t. salt
Garnish: paprika, fresh parsley

Tear bread into bite-size pieces. Alternate layers of bread and cheese in a slow cooker; set aside. Whisk together eggs, cream, evaporated milk, parsley and salt in a bowl; pour over bread and cheese. Sprinkle with paprika. Cover and cook on low setting for 3 to 4 hours. Garnish with parsley.

Cherylann Smith, *Efland, NC*

Farmhouse Pot Roast

After all day in the slow cooker, this roast is falling-apart tender and makes its own gravy.

Serves 6

3-lb. beef chuck roast
8-oz. pkg. whole mushrooms
16 new redskin potatoes
1/2 lb. carrots, peeled and sliced
3 stalks celery, chopped
14-oz. can beef broth
2 c. water
26-oz. can cream of mushroom soup
salt and pepper to taste
Optional: fresh parsley, chopped

Season roast with salt and pepper and brown on all sides in a skillet over high heat. Place roast in an ungreased slow cooker; top with vegetables. Blend together broth, water and soup in a medium bowl; pour over roast. Cover and cook on low setting for 6 to 8 hours, until roast is very tender. Garnish with parsley, if desired.

Farmhouse Pot Roast

Pat Wissler, *Harrisburg, PA*

No-Fuss Turkey Breast

With only three ingredients, prep time is amazingly fast.

Serves 6

5-lb. turkey breast
1.35-oz. pkg. onion soup mix
16-oz. can whole-berry cranberry sauce

Place turkey breast in a slow cooker. Combine soup mix and cranberry sauce in a bowl; spread over turkey. Cover and cook on low setting for 6 to 8 hours.

Connie Wagner, *Manchester, PA*

Pork & Rice in Tomato Sauce

My husband and my father both really love this meal.

Serves 4

30-oz. can tomato sauce
15-oz. can stewed tomatoes
1-3/4 to 2 c. water
1-1/2 c. long-cooking rice, uncooked
4 pork chops
salt and pepper to taste

Combine tomato sauce, stewed tomatoes with juice, water and rice in a slow cooker; mix well. Sprinkle chops with salt and pepper; add to slow cooker, pressing them down into the liquid. If they are not covered, add more water. Cover and cook on low setting for 6 to 8 hours, adding more water if needed.

Lisa Hains, *Tipp City, OH*

Smoky Sausage Dinner

For even simpler preparation, use canned small potatoes and cook just until everything is heated through.

Serves 4 to 6

1 lb. smoked sausage, cut into 1-inch pieces
6 to 8 potatoes, peeled and quartered
2 14-1/2 oz. cans French-style green beans, drained and juice of 1 can reserved
salt and garlic powder to taste

Brown sausage; drain. Arrange potatoes in a 5-quart slow cooker; top with green beans and reserved juice. Arrange sausage on top; sprinkle with salt and garlic powder. Cover and cook on high setting about 6 hours, until potatoes are tender.

Smoky Sausage Dinner

Kendall Hale, *Lynn, MA*

Coq Au Vin

Elegant enough for guests.

Serves 4

4 boneless, skinless chicken breasts
16-oz. pkg. sliced mushrooms
15-oz. jar pearl onions, drained
1/2 c. dry white wine or chicken broth
1 t. dried thyme
1 bay leaf
1 c. chicken broth
1/3 c. all-purpose flour
cooked rice
2 t. fresh parsley, chopped

Place chicken in a slow cooker; top with mushrooms and onions. Drizzle with wine or broth and sprinkle thyme over top; add bay leaf. Stir together broth and flour in a small bowl; pour into slow cooker. Cover and cook on low setting for 5 hours, or until juices run clear when chicken is pierced. Discard bay leaf. Serve over rice; sprinkle with parsley.

Sara Voges, *Washington, IN*

Daddy's Favorite Dinner

This is one of our summertime favorites, when the just-picked green beans turn up at the farmers' market!

Serves 4 to 6

14-oz. smoked turkey sausage ring, cut into serving-size pieces
1/2 onion, cut into chunks

10 new redskin potatoes
2 lbs. fresh green beans, trimmed and snapped
salt and pepper to taste
1 to 2 T. olive oil
Optional: 2 T. butter, sliced

Place all ingredients in a slow cooker; stir well. Cover and cook on high setting for 5 hours, or on low setting for 8 to 10 hours.

Jo Ann, *Gooseberry Patch*

Sweet & Sauerkraut Brats

Perfect for tailgating or a fall supper, these sandwiches go nicely with chips, fries or potato salad.

Serves 4 to 6

1-1/2 to 2 lbs. bratwurst, cut into bite-size pieces
27-oz. can sauerkraut
4 tart apples, cored, peeled and chopped
1/4 c. onion, chopped
1/4 c. brown sugar, packed
1 t. caraway seed
4 to 6 hard rolls, split
Optional: spicy mustard

Place bratwurst in a 5- to 6-quart slow cooker. Toss together sauerkraut, apple, onion, brown sugar and caraway seed; spoon over bratwurst. Cover and cook on high setting one hour; reduce heat to low setting and cook 2 to 3 more hours, stirring occasionally. Fill rolls, using a slotted spoon. Serve with mustard, if desired.

Sweet & Sauerkraut Brats

Shannon Kennedy, *Delaware, OH*

Newlywed Beef & Noodles

Enough for 2 plus some leftovers!

Serves 4

1 lb. stew beef cubes, browned
3 14-1/2 oz. cans beef broth
3 to 4 cubes beef bouillon
8-oz. pkg. egg noodles, uncooked

Add beef, broth and 3 broth cans of water to a slow cooker; stir in bouillon cubes. Cover and cook on low setting for 4 to 6 hours; add noodles. Cover and cook on low setting until noodles are done.

Linda Harmon, *Garner, NC*

Chicken Cordon Bleu

If you love traditional Chicken Cordon Bleu, give this easy slow-cooker version a try! Chicken, ham and Swiss cheese slow-simmered for hours in a creamy sauce...mmm.

Serves 4 to 6

10-3/4 oz. can cream of chicken soup
1 c. milk
4 to 6 boneless, skinless chicken breasts
1/4 lb. sliced deli ham
1/4 lb. sliced Swiss cheese

In a bowl, combine soup and milk. Pour enough of soup mixture into a slow cooker to cover the bottom; arrange chicken over top. Cover chicken with slices of ham and cheese. Pour remaining soup mixture over cheese. Cover and cook on low setting for 4 to 6 hours, or on high setting for 2 to 3 hours, until chicken is done.

Barbara Cordle, *London, OH*

Cheesy Chicken & Potatoes

My family asks for this recipe every time they have a chance to choose what's for dinner!

Serves 6 to 8

32-oz. pkg. frozen shredded hashbrowns
17-oz. pkg. frozen chopped broccoli
2 10-3/4 oz. cans Cheddar cheese soup
2 12-oz. cans evaporated milk
1-1/2 lbs. boneless, skinless chicken breasts, cubed
6-oz. can French-fried onions
salt and pepper to taste
12-oz. pkg. shredded Cheddar cheese

Combine hashbrowns, broccoli, soup, milk, chicken and onions in a 5-quart slow cooker sprayed with non-stick vegetable spray. Add salt and pepper to taste; stir well. Cover and cook on high setting for 4 hours, or on low setting for 8 to 9 hours. Stir in shredded cheese during the last 30 minutes of cooking time.

Cheesy Chicken & Potatoes

Stewed Chicken Verde

Robin Acasio, *Chula Vista, CA*

Stewed Chicken Verde

I love to use my slow-cooker and I'm always thinking up new ideas and flavors to try. This recipe was a hit with my family and I have been making it ever since!

Serves 4 to 6

3 to 3-1/2 lb. whole chicken
1 T. poultry seasoning
1/2 c. onion, sliced
several sprigs fresh cilantro
10-3/4 oz. can cream of chicken soup
4-oz. can chopped green chiles
cooked rice
Garnish: fresh cilantro sprigs, lime wedges

Sprinkle chicken all over with poultry seasoning. Place onion slices and cilantro sprigs inside chicken. Place chicken in an oval 4-quart slow cooker; top with soup and chiles. Cover and cook on low setting for 7 to 8 hours. Shred the chicken and serve with cooked rice. Garnish with cilantro and lime wedges.

Missy Frost, *Xenia, OH*

Missy's Easy Pork Roast

You won't believe how tender and delicious this roast is! It's wonderful with mashed potatoes.

Serves 4 to 6

2 to 3-lb. pork roast
1-1/2 oz. pkg. onion soup mix
3/4 to 1 c. milk
2 slices bacon, halved

Place roast in a slow cooker; set aside. Combine soup mix and milk in a bowl and spread over roast. Lay bacon slices on top of roast. Cover and cook on low setting for 6 to 8 hours.

Jamie Johnson, *Gooseberry Patch*

Bacon & Sage Roast Turkey

The easiest-ever Thanksgiving dinner...all you need to add is cranberry sauce and dessert!

Serves 8

8 new redskin potatoes, halved
1-1/2 c. baby carrots
1/2 t. garlic-pepper seasoning
6-lb. turkey breast
12-oz. jar roast turkey gravy
2 T. all-purpose flour
4 to 6 slices bacon, crisply cooked and crumbled
1 T. Worcestershire sauce
3/4 t. dried sage
Garnish: fresh sage

Arrange potatoes and carrots in a slow cooker; sprinkle with seasoning. Place turkey breast-side up on top of vegetables. Combine gravy, flour, bacon, Worcestershire sauce and sage in a small bowl. Mix well and pour over turkey and vegetables. Cover and cook on low setting for 7 to 9 hours, until juices run clear when turkey is pierced. Garnish with fresh sprigs of sage.

Molly Cool, *Marysville, OH*

Teriyaki Beef

This is the recipe I reach for when I find time's short!

Serves 4

1/3 c. teriyaki marinade
8-oz. can crushed pineapple
1-1/2 lb. boneless beef chuck steak
Optional: hot cooked noodles

Spray a slow cooker with non-stick vegetable spray; add marinade and pineapple with juice. Place steak in marinade mixture. Cover and cook on high setting for 2-1/2 to 3-1/2 hours. Serve over cooked noodles, if desired.

Nicole Manley, *Great Lakes, IL*

Penn Dutch Ham Potpie

When I was in elementary school, our school cafeteria made a version of this. As I got older, I decided it was time to recreate the memory! You can also substitute turkey or chicken.

Serves 6

1-lb. cooked ham steak, diced
6 c. water
3 to 4 potatoes, peeled and cubed
1 onion, chopped
1/2 c. celery, chopped
1/2 c. carrot, peeled and chopped
1 T. dried parsley
salt and pepper to taste

Add ham and water to a large slow cooker. Cover and cook on low setting for 5 hours. Add remaining ingredients. Cover and cook on low setting for 2 hours longer, or until vegetables are tender. About 15 minutes before serving, add Potpie Squares; stir. Cover and cook for 15 minutes longer, or until squares are fully cooked.

Potpie Squares:

1 egg, beaten
2 to 4 T. water
pepper to taste
1 c. all-purpose flour

In a large bowl, whisk together egg, water and pepper. Add flour, a little at a time, until a soft dough forms. On a floured surface, roll out dough 1/4-inch thick. With a sharp knife, cut into 2-inch squares.

Amy Blanchard, *Hazel Park, MI*

Company Chicken & Stuffing

Try Cheddar or brick cheese for a tasty variation in flavor.

Serves 4

4 boneless, skinless chicken breasts
4 slices Swiss cheese
6-oz. pkg. chicken-flavored stuffing mix
2 10-3/4 oz. cans cream of chicken soup
1/2 c. chicken broth

Arrange chicken in a 4-quart slow cooker; top each piece with a slice of cheese. Combine stuffing mix, soup and broth in a bowl; spoon into slow cooker. Cover and cook on low setting for 6 to 8 hours.

Company Chicken & Stuffing

Potato-Corn Chowder

Jerry Bostian, *Oelwein, IA*

Potato-Corn Chowder

Short on time? Use a package of ready-cooked bacon instead.

Serves 6 to 8

2 10-3/4 oz. cans potato soup
2 14-3/4 oz. cans cream-style corn
8 slices bacon, crisply cooked and crumbled,
    1 to 2 T. drippings reserved
1/2 to 1 c. milk
salt, pepper and garlic salt to taste
Garnish: fresh parsley, chopped

Blend soup and corn in a 4-quart slow cooker; add bacon along with bacon drippings, if desired. Add milk until soup is of desired consistency; add salt, pepper and garlic salt to taste. Cover and cook on low setting for 8 to 10 hours. Sprinkle individual servings with parsley.

Glenda Tolbert, *Moore, SC*

Winter Steak Kabobs

Toss everything in the slow cooker before you head out for your holiday shopping. Serve with a tossed salad and garlic bread when you get back! Who needs a grill?

Serves 2 to 4

1-lb. beef sirloin tip steak, cubed
2 14-1/2 oz. cans whole potatoes, drained

salt and pepper to taste
1 green pepper, sliced
1 onion, sliced
15-1/4 oz. can pineapple chunks, drained
18-oz. bottle barbecue sauce

Place steak and potatoes in a slow cooker; sprinkle with salt and pepper. Add pepper, onion and pineapple; cover with barbecue sauce. Cover and cook on low setting for 6 hours, or high setting for 4 hours, until steak and vegetables are tender.

Candace Whitelock, *Seaford, DE*

Nacho Chicken & Rice

Make wraps by spooning into flour tortillas, folding over and rolling up from the bottom.

Serves 6 to 8

1 lb. boneless, skinless chicken breasts, cubed
2 10-3/4 oz. cans Cheddar cheese soup
16-oz. jar chunky salsa
1-1/4 c. water
1-1/4 c. long-cooking rice, uncooked

Combine all ingredients in a slow cooker. Cover and cook on low setting for about 5 hours, until chicken and rice are tender.

Handy Tip

Want to change the cooking time of a slow cooker recipe? It's simple...one hour of cooking on high equals 2 to 2-1/2 hours on low.

Reuben Bake

Dorothy McConnell, *Brooklyn, IA*

Reuben Bake

Celebrate St. Patrick's Day with this easy slow-cooker casserole inspired by the classic Reuben deli sandwich!

Serves 6 to 8

16-oz. pkg. wide egg noodles, cooked and divided
12-oz. can corned beef, drained, chopped and
 divided
3-1/2 c. sauerkraut
6 slices American cheese
16-oz. container sour cream
10-3/4 oz. can cream of chicken soup
6 slices Swiss cheese

In a greased 4-quart slow cooker, layer half the noodles; top with half the corned beef. Top with all the sauerkraut and all the American cheese. Stir together sour cream and soup; spoon half of sour cream mixture over American cheese. Layer with remaining noodles, corned beef and sour cream mixture; top with Swiss cheese. Cover and cook on high setting for 2 hours, or until hot and bubbly. Reduce setting to low; cover and cook for one to 2 hours longer. Before serving, stir to combine layers.

Vicki Snyder, *Santa Maria, CA*

Chicken Adobo

When I was a girl growing up in Guadalupe, a farming community along the central coast of California, my mom made me this wonderful dish every year for my birthday.

Serves 8

1 onion, sliced
7 to 8 cloves garlic, pressed
2 T. cracked pepper
2 bay leaves
3 to 3-1/2 lbs. chicken thighs and drumsticks
1 c. white vinegar
1 c. soy sauce
cooked short-grain white rice

Place onion in a slow cooker. Wrap garlic, pepper and bay leaves in cheesecloth; tie with kitchen string or place in a tea strainer. Add spice bundle to slow cooker. Add chicken. In a small bowl, mix vinegar and soy sauce. Pour over chicken. Cover and cook on low setting for 4 to 6 hours, stirring occasionally, until chicken juices run clear. Discard spice bundle before serving. Serve over rice.

Claire Bertram, *Lexington, KY*

Sweet & Spicy Country Ham

This ham brings back memories of Christmas at Grandma's house.

Serves 12

6-lb. bone-in country ham
30 whole cloves
3 c. apple cider, divided
1 c. brown sugar, packed
1 c. maple syrup
2 T. cinnamon
2 T. ground cloves
1 T. nutmeg
2 t. ground ginger
zest of 1 orange
Optional: 1 T. vanilla extract

Make shallow cuts in fat on outside of ham one inch apart in a diamond pattern. Insert cloves in centers of diamonds; place in a 6- to 7-quart slow cooker. Pour in enough cider to cover all but top 2 inches of ham. Pack brown sugar over top of ham, pressing firmly; drizzle with syrup. Sprinkle with spices, zest and vanilla, if desired. Add remaining cider without going over fill line. Cover and cook on low setting for 8 to 10 hours.

Lynda Robson, *Boston, MA*

Slow-Cooker Sloppy Joes

These joes are an easy picnic lunch.

Serves 14 to 18

3 c. celery, chopped
1 c. onion, chopped
1 c. catsup
1 c. barbecue sauce
1 c. water
2 T. vinegar
2 T. Worcestershire sauce
2 T. brown sugar, packed
1 t. chili powder
1 t. salt
1 t. pepper
1/2 t. garlic powder
3 to 4-lb. boneless chuck roast
14 to 18 hamburger buns
Garnishes: banana peppers, sliced olives, carrot crinkles, pretzel sticks, sliced pimentos, fresh parsley sprigs

Combine the first 12 ingredients in a 4- to 5-quart slow cooker; mix well. Add roast; cover and cook on high setting 6 to 7 hours, until tender. Remove roast; shred meat, return to slow cooker and heat through. Serve on hamburger buns. Garnish as desired.

Slow-Cooker Sloppy Joes

Cabbage Patch

Jennifer Crisp, *Abingdon, IL*

Cabbage Patch

Old-fashioned comfort food at its best, and this recipe feeds a crowd! Leftovers, if you have any, freeze wonderfully.

Serves 10

1-1/2 lbs. ground beef
1 onion, diced
2 14-1/2 oz. cans diced tomatoes
2 15-oz. cans kidney beans, drained and rinsed
2 14-oz. cans beef broth
3 stalks celery, diced
3 potatoes, peeled and diced
4 carrots, peeled and diced
1 head cabbage, chopped
1 T. sugar
ground cumin, garlic powder, pepper and onion
    salt to taste

In a skillet over medium heat, brown beef and onion; drain. Add beef mixture to a slow cooker; add tomatoes with juice and remaining ingredients. Mix well. Cover and cook on low setting for 4 to 5 hours, until vegetables are soft.

—— *Handy Tip* ——

To make sure your meal is finished in the time listed on your recipe, and to avoid undercooking, don't overfill your slow cooker.

Marlene Darnell, *Newport Beach, CA*

Country Captain

We discovered this curry-flavored dish with the unusual name on a trip to southern Georgia.

Serves 4

2 T. olive oil
3-lb. chicken, quartered and skin removed
2 cloves garlic, minced
1 onion, chopped
1 green pepper, chopped
1/2 c. celery, chopped
2 t. curry powder
1/3 c. currants or raisins
14-1/2 oz. can whole tomatoes, chopped
1 t. sugar
salt and pepper to taste
hot cooked rice
Garnish: 1/4 c. slivered almonds

Heat oil in a skillet over medium heat. Sauté chicken just until golden; place in a 4- to 5-quart slow cooker and set aside. Add garlic, onion, green pepper, celery and curry powder to skillet; sauté briefly. Remove from heat; stir in remaining ingredients except rice and almonds. Pour over chicken. Cover and cook on low setting for 6 hours, or until chicken is no longer pink. Serve over cooked rice; garnish with almonds.

Rhonda Reeder, *Ellicott City, MD*

Slow-Cooker Chicken & Dumplings

With a slow cooker, you can serve your family a homestyle dinner even after a busy day away from home.

Serves 8

1-1/2 lbs. boneless, skinless chicken breasts, cubed
2 potatoes, cubed
2 c. baby carrots
2 stalks celery, sliced
2 10-3/4 oz. cans cream of chicken soup
1 c. water
1 t. dried thyme
1/4 t. pepper
2 c. biscuit baking mix
2/3 c. milk

Place chicken, potatoes, carrots and celery in a slow cooker; set aside. In a medium bowl, combine soup, water, thyme and pepper; pour over chicken mixture. Cover and cook on low setting 7 to 8 hours, until juices run clear when chicken is pierced. Mix together baking mix and milk; drop into slow cooker by large spoonfuls. Tilt lid to vent and cook on high setting 30 minutes, or until dumplings are cooked in center.

Jean Yeager, *New Castle, PA*

Fettuccine & Pepperoni

I often make this recipe when we're camping...I just use a can of evaporated milk in place of the cream. We love this simple and budget-friendly dish!

Serves 6 to 8

4 eggs
1/4 c. whipping cream or 5-oz. can evaporated milk
16-oz. pkg. fettuccine pasta, cooked
1/2 c. butter, softened
8-oz. pkg. sliced pepperoni
1 c. grated Parmesan cheese
1/4 c. fresh parsley, chopped

In a bowl, beat together eggs and cream or milk until well blended. In a slow cooker, toss warm pasta with butter and pepperoni. Pour egg mixture over top; stir. Cover and cook on low setting for 4 to 6 hours, until set. Before serving, sprinkle with Parmesan cheese and parsley.

Fettuccine & Pepperoni

Cranberry Corned Beef

April Jacobs, *Loveland, CO*

Cranberry Corned Beef

The cranberry glaze against the fresh parsley is so beautiful.

Serves 6 to 8

4-lb. cured corned beef brisket with spice
    packet
5 large carrots, peeled and cut into 3-inch
    pieces
1 onion, cut into 6 wedges
14-oz. can whole-berry cranberry sauce
14-oz. can jellied cranberry sauce
2 1-oz. pkgs. onion soup mix
1/2 c. sour cream
4 t. prepared horseradish
1/4 t. pepper
Garnish: fresh parsley, chopped

Trim fat from brisket. Place carrots and onion in a slow cooker; place brisket on top of vegetables. Sprinkle spice packet over brisket. Combine cranberry sauces and soup mix in a bowl. Spoon over brisket. Cover and cook on high setting for one hour. Reduce heat to low setting and cook for 8 hours. Meanwhile, combine sour cream and horseradish in a small bowl. Cover and chill until ready to serve. Transfer brisket to a serving platter. Spoon carrots, onion and, if desired, a little cooking liquid around brisket on platter. Serve with sauce. Sprinkle with pepper. Garnish with parsley.

Kathy Lowe, *Orem, UT*

Mexicali Beef Soft Tacos

Two meals in one! You can make tacos the first night, then warm the remaining meat with barbecue sauce for sandwiches another night.

Serves 10 to 12

1/2 to 1 c. water
4 to 5-lb. beef chuck roast
1/2 red onion, chopped
3 cloves garlic, peeled
1/4 c. oil
1 T. red pepper flakes
2 t. ground cumin
2 t. dried oregano
1 t. pepper
10 to 12 10-inch corn or flour tortillas, warmed
Garnish: shredded lettuce, chopped onion,
    chopped tomatoes, sour cream, salsa

Pour water into a slow cooker; add roast and set aside. Combine onion, garlic, oil and seasonings in a blender. Blend until mixed; pour over roast. Cover and cook on high setting for about 7 hours, until roast is very tender. Shred roast with 2 forks; return to slow cooker. Reduce heat to low setting. Cover and cook for one more hour. Fill tortillas with beef mixture; add toppings as desired.

Suzette Rummell, *Cuyahoga Falls, OH*

Beef Tips & Noodles

An old family favorite.

Serves 6

3 to 4-lb. beef chuck roast, cubed
salt and pepper to taste
10-3/4 oz. can golden mushroom soup
10-3/4 oz. can cream of mushroom soup
2-1/2 c. water
0.53-oz. pkg. French onion soup mix
2 T. all-purpose flour
3 T. cold water
8-oz. container sour cream
8-oz. pkg. medium egg noodles, cooked

Season beef with salt and pepper; place in a 6-quart slow cooker. Stir together soups, 2-1/2 cups water and soup mix in a bowl; add to slow cooker. Cover and cook on high for 6 to 7 hours, until beef is tender. Stir flour into 3 tablespoons cold water in a small bowl; add to slow cooker, stirring gently. Cover and cook on high about 15 minutes, until gravy is desired consistency. Stir in sour cream. Serve over cooked noodles.

~Handy Tip~

Add hardy herbs like thyme and rosemary to dishes early in the cooking process; this way, you'll achieve maximum flavor and less intrusive texture.

Vickie, *Gooseberry Patch*

Slow-Cooker Chicken with Rice

Slow cooking keeps the chicken oh-so tender and moist.

Serves 4

4 boneless, skinless chicken breasts
1/4 t. salt
1/4 t. pepper
1/4 t. paprika
1 T. oil
14-1/2 oz. can crushed tomatoes
1 red pepper, chopped
1 onion, chopped
1 clove garlic, minced
1/2 t. dried rosemary
10-oz. pkg. frozen peas
cooked rice

Sprinkle chicken with seasonings; set aside. Heat oil in a medium skillet over medium-high heat; add chicken and cook until golden on all sides. Arrange chicken in a slow cooker. In a small bowl, combine remaining ingredients except peas and rice; pour over chicken. Cover and cook on low setting 7 to 9 hours, or on high setting 3 to 4 hours. One hour before serving, stir in peas. Serve over rice.

Slow-Cooker Chicken with Rice

Chapter Four

Surprises from the Slow Cooker

Slow cookers that do more than slow cook!
Every day, cooks are coming up with new and creative ways to make amazing food in their slow cookers! It's such a surprise to find that you can bake in your slow cooker and make goodies like Delectable Lemon Cheesecake or Mrs. Finnegan's Pumpkin Tea Bread. Or that you can cook recipes like Country Corn Pudding or Spoon Bread Florentine. But the sweetest surprises are coffee barista-style drinks like Pumpkin Spice Latte and gourmet candies like Chocolatey Peanut Butter Pretzel Drops. In this chapter, you'll find a surprise hidden on every page!

Annette Ingram, *Grand Rapids, MI*

Slow-Cooker Swiss Tomato Toddy

After an afternoon on the ski slopes, a mug of this bracing beverage is always welcome!

Serves 6

46-oz. can tomato juice
8-oz. can tomato sauce
3 cubes beef or vegetable bouillon
1/2 c. boiling water
3 whole peppercorns
1/2 bay leaf
1/4 t. dried basil
1/2 onion, thinly sliced
2 T. sugar
2 whole cloves

Combine all ingredients in a slow cooker; mix well. Cover and cook on low setting for 7 to 8 hours, until hot. Strain and discard whole spices before serving.

Dana Cunningham, *Lafayette, LA*

Ham & Swiss Quiche

Quiche is the perfect protein for breakfast, lunch or dinner!

Serves 6

14.1-oz. pkg. refrigerated pie crusts
2 c. shredded Swiss cheese, divided
1 c. cooked ham, chopped
4 green onions, chopped
6 eggs
1 c. whipping cream
1/4 t. salt
1/4 t. pepper
1/8 t. nutmeg

Cut pie crusts in half. Press 3 pie crust halves into bottom and 2 inches up sides of a greased oval slow cooker, overlapping seams by 1/4 inch. Reserve remaining pie crust half for another use. Cover and cook on high setting for 1-1/2 hours. Sprinkle one cup cheese, ham and green onions over crust. Whisk together eggs and remaining ingredients in a medium bowl; pour over ingredients in crust. Sprinkle remaining one cup cheese over egg mixture. Cover and cook on high setting for 1-1/2 hours, or until filling is set. Uncover and let stand 5 minutes before serving. Cut quiche into wedges; serve immediately.

Ham & Swiss Quiche

Apple-Cinnamon Bread in Jars

Dale Duncan, *Waterloo, IA*

Apple-Cinnamon Bread in Jars

Topped with a little apple butter, slices of this bread are out-of-this-world good!

Makes 2 loaves

1 c. all-purpose flour
1-1/2 t. baking powder
1 t. cinnamon
1/4 t. salt
1/2 c. brown sugar, packed
2 T. butter, softened
2 eggs, lightly beaten
1/4 c. cinnamon applesauce
1 Gala apple, peeled, cored and diced
1/2 c. chopped walnuts
1/2 c. warm water

In a bowl, combine flour, baking powder, cinnamon and salt; mix well and set aside. In a separate bowl, mix together brown sugar, butter, eggs, applesauce and apple; mix well. Stir in walnuts. Add sugar mixture to flour mixture and mix well until moistened. Evenly spoon mixture into 2 greased and floured wide-mouth canning jars. Cover jars with lightly greased aluminum foil. Place jars in a slow cooker; pour 1/2 cup warm water around jars. Cover and cook on high setting for 1-1/2 to 2 hours, until a toothpick tests clean. Remove jars from slow cooker. Let cool for 10 minutes before turning out loaves.

Rhonda Reeder, *Ellicott City, MD*

Meatless Stuffed Peppers

My pals from card club rave about these delicious peppers! They cook best in an oval slow cooker.

Makes 6 servings

2 c. cooked brown rice
3 tomatoes, chopped
1 c. frozen corn, thawed
1 sweet onion, chopped
1/3 c. canned kidney beans, drained and rinsed
1/3 c. canned black beans, drained and rinsed
3/4 c. Monterey Jack cheese, cubed
4-1/4 oz. can chopped black olives, drained
3 cloves garlic, minced
1 t. salt
1/2 t. pepper
6 green, red or yellow peppers, tops removed
3/4 c. spaghetti sauce
1/2 c. water

In a large bowl, combine rice, tomatoes, corn, onion and beans. Stir in cheese, olives, garlic, salt and pepper. Spoon into peppers. Combine spaghetti sauce and water. Pour half of sauce mixture into an oval 6-quart slow cooker. Place stuffed peppers on top. Pour remaining sauce over peppers. Cover and cook on low setting for 3-1/2 to 4 hours, until peppers are tender.

Ellie Brandel, *Clackamas, OR*

Banana Bread

Keep it simple. If you don't have half-and-half, you can use an equal amount of evaporated milk instead, and a small loaf pan can be used if your slow cooker is oval.

Makes one loaf

1/3 c. shortening
1/2 c. sugar
2 eggs
1-3/4 c. all-purpose flour
1 t. baking powder
1/2 t. baking soda
1/2 t. salt
1 c. bananas, mashed
1/2 c. raisins

Blend together shortening and sugar in a mixing bowl; add eggs and beat well. Combine flour, baking powder, baking soda and salt in a separate bowl. Add dry ingredients alternately with bananas; stir in raisins. Pour batter into a greased 4-cup metal coffee can. Cover top of can with 6 to 8 paper towels to absorb condensation; set on a rack in a slow cooker. Cover and cook on high setting for 2 to 3 hours, until bread is done. Let cool slightly; turn out of can to finish cooling.

Darrell Lawry, *Kissimmee, FL*

Chocolatey Peanut Butter Pretzel Drops

My go-to recipe for gifts...it's always requested by friends, neighbors and co-workers!

Makes about 4 dozen pieces

10-oz. jar salted dry-roasted peanuts
2 11-1/2 oz. pkgs. semi-sweet chocolate chips
1/2 c. creamy peanut butter
24-oz. pkg. melting chocolate, chopped or
   broken up
2-1/2 c. pretzels, chopped or broken up

Layer all ingredients in a slow cooker. Cover and cook on high setting for one hour, stirring occasionally, or until chocolate is melted. Stir again until smooth. Drop by tablespoonfuls onto wax paper; let stand until set. Store in an airtight container.

Chocolatey Peanut Butter Pretzel Drops

Cinnamon Rolls

Peggy Pelfrey, *Ashland City, TN*

Cinnamon Rolls

This recipe is easy to make for a leisurely brunch or a sleep-in Saturday or Sunday morning. The house fills with the delicious smell of cinnamon rolls...yummy!

Serves 8

1/4 c. butter, melted
1 t. vanilla extract
1/2 c. brown sugar, packed
1 T. plus 1 t. cinnamon, divided
12-oz. can refrigerated biscuits
Optional: chopped pecans
1-1/3 c. powdered sugar
2 T. milk

In a small bowl, mix together melted butter and vanilla; set aside. In a separate bowl, combine brown sugar and one teaspoon cinnamon. Roll biscuits in butter mixture, then in brown sugar mixture until well coated. Place biscuits in a slow cooker lightly sprayed with non-stick cooking spray; sprinkle with pecans, if using. Place a paper towel on top of slow cooker and cover with lid. Cook on low setting for 2 to 3 hours. Meanwhile, mix together powdered sugar, milk and remaining cinnamon in a small bowl. When rolls are done, drizzle with glaze.

Regina Vining, *Warwick, RI*

Spiced Chocolate Coffee

This sweet sipper is conveniently made in a slow cooker. Top with sweetened whipped cream for a special treat.

Makes about 8 cups

8 c. brewed coffee
1/3 c. sugar
1/2 c. chocolate syrup
4 4-inch cinnamon sticks, broken
1 t. whole cloves
Garnish: cinnamon sticks, sweetened whipped
    cream

Combine first 3 ingredients in a 3-quart slow cooker; set aside. Wrap spices in a coffee filter or cheesecloth and tie with kitchen string; add to slow cooker. Cover and cook on low setting for 2 to 3 hours. Remove and discard spices. Ladle coffee into mugs and garnish.

Satoko Harjo, *Edmonds, WA*

Hawaiian Ham Sammies

My friends and I get together and exchange frozen dinners. Hawaiian Ham Sammies is the most-requested main dish!

Serves 8

2 lbs. cooked ham, thinly sliced
1/4 c. onion, chopped
1 c. catsup
1/2 c. water
1/2 c. vinegar
1/4 c. mustard
1/4 c. plus 2 T. brown sugar, packed
2 T. Worcestershire sauce
8 Kaiser rolls, split
15-1/4 oz. can pineapple slices, drained

Combine all ingredients except rolls and pineapple in a slow cooker. Cover and cook on low setting for 6 to 8 hours. Serve ham mixture on split rolls, topped with pineapple slices.

Chad Rutan, *Gooseberry Patch*

Bacon-Wrapped Egg Cups

These tasty little breakfast cups are a hit at breakfast time. We serve them on top of thick toast slices with a few sprinkles of hot sauce or catsup.

Serves 6

6 slices thick-cut peppered bacon
6 eggs, beaten
1 c. sliced mushrooms
3 roma tomatoes, diced
1 green pepper, diced
1 t. garlic, minced
salt and pepper to taste

Cook bacon in a skillet over medium heat until almost crisp; drain on paper towels. Scramble eggs to desired doneness in drippings in skillet; set aside. In a bowl, combine vegetables and garlic; season with salt and pepper. Lightly grease 6 small ramekins or custard dishes. Arrange one slice of bacon around the inside of each ramekin. Evenly spoon egg mixture and vegetables into ramekins. Place a trivet in a slow cooker; put ramekins on trivet. Add water to slow cooker to a depth of about one inch. Cover and cook on high setting for 1-1/2 to 2 hours, until warmed through and vegetables are tender.

Bacon-Wrapped Egg Cups

Delectable Lemon Cheesecake

Cheri Maxwell, *Gulf Breeze, FL*

Delectable Lemon Cheesecake

With all the delicious excesses of holiday meals and occasions, a light-tasting dessert is very welcome! I like to serve slices of this cheesecake garnished with a puff of whipped cream and a twist of lemon peel.

Serves 8

1 c. vanilla wafers, crumbled
3 T. butter, melted
2/3 c. plus 1 T. sugar, divided
1-1/2 t. lemon zest, divided
2 8-oz. pkgs. cream cheese, softened
2 eggs
1 T. all-purpose flour
2 T. lemon juice

In a bowl, combine vanilla wafer crumbs, melted butter, one tablespoon sugar and 1/2 teaspoon lemon zest. Pat into a 7" round springform pan; set aside. In a separate bowl, beat together cream cheese and remaining sugar with an electric mixer on medium speed until smooth. Add eggs; beat for 3 minutes. Add flour, lemon juice and remaining lemon zest; continue beating for one minute. Pour filling into crust. Set pan on a trivet in a slow cooker. Cover and cook on high setting for 2-1/2 to 3 hours. Turn off slow cooker; let stand, covered, for one to 2 hours. Remove pan from slow cooker; cool completely before removing sides of pan. Cover and chill until serving time.

Tiffany Brinkley, *Broomfield, CO*

Easy Brown Bread

Serve hot and top with lots of butter!

Makes one loaf

2 c. whole-wheat flour
1 c. all-purpose flour
1 T. baking powder
1 t. salt
2 T. molasses
2 T. oil
1-1/3 c. water

Combine flours, baking powder and salt in a large bowl; stir to mix. Add molasses, oil and 1-1/3 cups water; mix until moistened. Place batter in a greased 5-quart slow cooker. Place 5 paper towels across top of slow cooker to catch any condensation. Cover, placing a wooden toothpick between paper towels and lid to allow steam to escape. Cook on high setting 2 hours; do not uncover while cooking. Loosen sides of bread with a knife; remove from slow cooker and place on a wire rack.

Valerie Sholes, *Minneapolis, MN*

Bacon & Cheese Breakfast Casserole

This casserole is full of lots of tasty breakfast favorites...sure to please even the pickiest of eaters.

Serves 8 to 10

1 T. oil
1 onion, chopped
32-oz. pkg. frozen shredded hashbrowns, thawed
1 green pepper, chopped
1/2 lb. bacon, crisply cooked and crumbled
8-oz. pkg. shredded Cheddar cheese
8-oz. pkg. shredded mozzarella cheese
1 doz. eggs
1 c. skim milk
1 T. dried parsley
1 t. dry mustard
2 t. salt
1 t. pepper
Optional: additional shredded Cheddar cheese

Heat oil in a skillet over medium heat. Sauté onion in oil until translucent. Stir in hashbrowns and cook until golden. Place half the hashbrown mixture in a lightly greased slow cooker. Top hashbrown mixture with green pepper, bacon and cheeses; set aside. In a bowl, beat together eggs, milk, parsley, mustard, salt and pepper. Pour egg mixture over cheese in slow cooker. Cover and cook on low setting for 5 to 6 hours, until a knife tip tests clean. Sprinkle a little extra cheese on servings, if desired.

David Wink, *Gooseberry Patch*

Championship Cheese Dip

A few years ago, I whipped this up before our biggest football rivalry game. We won the game and went on to win the National Championship. Now, I make it for every game!

Makes 20 to 25 servings

1 lb. ground beef, browned and drained
1/2 lb. spicy pork sausage, browned and drained
32-oz. pkg. pasteurized process cheese spread, cubed
2 10-oz. cans diced tomatoes with green chiles
tortilla chips

Combine all ingredients except chips in a slow cooker; mix well. Cover and cook on low setting for 4 hours, or until the cheese is melted, stirring occasionally. Serve with tortilla chips.

Tina Hockensmith, *Canton, OH*

Hot Dog Topping

This tasty topping is a "must" at our cookouts!

Serves 6 to 8

1 lb. ground beef, browned and drained
32-oz. pkg. refrigerated sauerkraut, drained
2 c. tomato juice
1/2 c. brown sugar, packed
salt and pepper to taste

Add all ingredients to a slow cooker; stir well. Cover and cook on low to medium setting for 2 hours, or until heated through.

Championship Cheese Dip

Spoon Bread Florentine

Vickie, *Gooseberry Patch*

Spoon Bread Florentine

Robust with flavor.

Makes 8 servings

10-oz. pkg. frozen chopped spinach, thawed
  and drained
6 green onions, sliced
1 red pepper, chopped
5-1/2 oz. pkg. cornbread mix
4 eggs, beaten
1/2 c. butter, melted
1 c. cottage cheese
1-1/4 t. seasoned salt

Combine all ingredients in a large bowl; mix well. Spoon into a lightly greased slow cooker. Cover, with lid slightly ajar to allow moisture to escape. Cook on low setting for 3 to 4 hours, or on high setting for 1-3/4 to 2 hours, until edges are golden and a knife tip inserted in center tests clean.

Crystal Faulkner, *Asheboro, NC*

Best-Ever Hot Cocoa

My whole family looks forward to my special hot cocoa made in the slow cooker. Everyone who has tried this recipe swears it's the best ever, and I have to agree!

Serves 8 to 10

1-1/2 c. whipping cream
14-oz. can sweetened condensed milk

2 c. milk chocolate chips
6 c. milk
1 t. vanilla extract

Combine all ingredients in a slow cooker. Cover and cook on low setting for 2 hours, stirring occasionally. Ladle into mugs; serve warm.

Michelle Marberry, *Valley, AL*

Caramel Apple Cider

Tailgaters and trick-or-treaters love this drink on a crisp fall night!

8 servings

64-oz. bottle apple cider
1/2 c. caramel ice cream topping
1/2 t. cinnamon
Garnish: whipped cream, cinnamon,
  additional caramel topping, cinnamon sticks

Combine all ingredients except garnish in a slow cooker. Cover and cook on low setting for 3 to 4 hours. Ladle hot cider into mugs; top with a dollop of whipped cream, a sprinkle of cinnamon and a drizzle of caramel topping. Serve with a cinnamon stick for stirring.

— *Handy Tip* —
Breads baked in a slow cooker won't actually brown or develop a crust. If you like, broil the loaf for a few minutes after removing it from the slow cooker.

Country Corn Pudding

Angela Lively, *Baxter, TN*

Country Corn Pudding

With four kinds of corn, this new twist on an old favorite is scrumptious!

Serves 8

16-oz. pkg. frozen corn
2 11-oz. cans sweet corn & diced peppers
14-3/4 oz. can creamed corn
6-1/2 oz. pkg. corn muffin mix
3/4 c. water
1/4 c. butter, melted
1 t. salt
Garnish: fresh parsley, chopped

Mix all ingredients except garnish well in a large bowl; pour into a slow cooker. Cover and cook on low setting for 5 to 6 hours, stirring after 3 hours. Garnish with fresh parsley.

Jo Ann, *Gooseberry Patch*

Slow-Cooker Chai

Your overnight holiday guests will love waking up to this pleasing hot morning drink!

Serves 8 to 10

3-1/2 qts. water
1/2 to 3/4 c. sugar
15 slices fresh ginger, peeled
36 whole cardamom seeds, pods discarded
25 whole cloves
5 4-inch cinnamon sticks
3 whole black peppercorns
8 black tea bags
14-oz. can sweetened condensed milk

Pour water into a slow cooker. Stir in sugar and spices. Cover and cook on high setting for up to 8 hours. Shortly before serving, steep tea bags in the hot liquid in the slow cooker for 5 minutes. Remove tea bags; strain whole spices. Stir in milk; serve hot.

Michelle Tucker, *Hamilton, OH*

Hot Apple Punch

What a wonderful warm drink for autumn. Plus, it makes your home smell simply delightful!

Serves 12

2 qts. apple juice
1-1/2 c. cranberry juice cocktail
1/2 c. brown sugar, packed
1/2 t. salt
4 4-inch cinnamon sticks
2 whole cloves
Garnish: 1 orange, sliced

Combine all ingredients except orange slices in a slow cooker. Cover and cook on low setting for 2 hours, or until brown sugar is dissolved and mixture is hot. Strain cinnamon sticks and cloves before serving; top with orange slices.

Michelle Marberry, *Valley, AL*

Hot Lemonade

Not medicine, but it sure feels good on a scratchy winter throat.

Makes 9 servings

4 c. water
juice of 14 lemons, or 3 c. lemon juice
2 c. sugar
1/4 c. honey
Garnish: cinnamon sticks

Combine all ingredients except garnish in a slow cooker. Cover and cook on low setting for 3 hours. Whisk well. Ladle into mugs; serve with cinnamon sticks for stirring.

Dana Cunningham, *Lafayette, LA*

Florida Orange Cheesecake

A citrusy cheesecake...I can't get enough of its unique flavor! Tastes amazing with a hot mug of coffee or mulled cider.

Serves 8 to 10

1-1/2 c. reduced-fat cream cheese, softened
1 T. all-purpose flour
1/2 c. sugar
2 T. orange juice
1/2 t. vanilla extract
3 eggs, lightly beaten
1/2 c. non-fat sour cream
1 t. orange zest
1 c. warm water
Optional: orange zest curls

In a large bowl, combine cream cheese, flour, sugar, juice and vanilla. Beat cream cheese mixture with an electric mixer on medium speed until combined; beat in eggs until smooth. Mix in sour cream until smooth; stir in zest. Spoon filling into a lightly greased 1-1/2 quart casserole dish; cover tightly with aluminum foil. Pour warm water into a large slow cooker; set casserole dish in water. Cover and cook on high setting for 2-1/2 hours, or until center of cheesecake is set. Carefully remove casserole dish to a wire rack; uncover and cool cheesecake. When cool, cover and refrigerate for 4 hours. Garnish slices with curls of orange zest, if desired.

Florida Orange Cheesecake

Janis Parr, *Ontario, Canada*

Wholesome Whole-Wheat Bread

This delicious bread is so easy to make with a no-fuss slow-cooker recipe. Served with homemade apple butter or strawberry preserves, warm slices of this bread are sure to win you over.

Makes one loaf

2 c. warm milk
2 T. oil
1/4 c. brown sugar, packed
1/2 t. salt
1 env. quick-rise dry yeast
1-1/4 c. all-purpose flour, divided
2-1/2 c. whole-wheat flour, divided

Heat milk until warm, about 110 to 115 degrees. In a bowl, combine warm milk, oil, brown sugar, salt, yeast, 3/4 cup all-purpose flour and 1-1/4 cups whole-wheat flour. Beat with an electric mixer on low speed for 2 minutes. Stir in remaining flour; mix well. Transfer dough to a lightly greased 9"x5" loaf pan; cover loosely with lightly greased aluminum foil. Let stand for 5 minutes; place in a large slow cooker. Cover and cook on high setting for 2-1/2 to 3 hours. Uncover and cool bread in pan on a wire rack.

Connie Hilty, *Pearland, TX*

Triple Chocolate-Nut Clusters

Candy making has never been so easy! The slow cooker is the perfect tool to keep this candy mixture warm while you're spooning it out.

Makes 6 dozen

16-oz. jar dry-roasted peanuts
9-3/4 oz. can salted whole cashews
2 c. pecan pieces
18 2-oz. chocolate bark coating squares, cut in half
12-oz. package semi-sweet chocolate morsels
4 1-oz. bittersweet chocolate baking squares, broken into pieces
1 T. shortening
1 t. vanilla extract

Combine all ingredients except vanilla in a 5-quart slow cooker; cover and cook on low setting 2 hours or until chocolate is melted. Stir in vanilla. Drop candy by heaping teaspoonfuls onto wax paper. Let stand at least 2 hours, or until firm. Store in an airtight container.

Triple Chocolate-Nut Clusters

Tennessee Mud Cake in a Can

Charlotte Crockett, *Palmyra, TN*

Tennessee Mud Cake in a Can

Mix up the flavor of this tasty cake by using peanut butter or white chocolate chips instead of the semi-sweet ones.

Serves 4 to 6

2 c. chocolate cake mix
1/2 c. instant chocolate pudding mix
2 c. sour cream
4 eggs, beaten
1 c. water
3/4 c. oil
1-1/2 c. semi-sweet chocolate chips
Garnish: chocolate ice cream

In a bowl, combine dry mixes, sour cream, eggs, water and oil; mix well until smooth. Stir in chocolate chips. Spoon batter into a greased 32-ounce metal coffee can. Set can in a slow cooker. Cover and cook on low setting for 3 to 4 hours, until a toothpick inserted in the center of cake comes out with moist crumbs. Top scoops of cake with a scoop of chocolate ice cream.

⟿ Change it Up ⟿

No need to peel the apples when you're cooking in that crock. The slow moist heat softens up the peels, and creates the perfect end result.

JoAnn, *Gooseberry Patch*

Maple French Toast Casserole

My family loves this super-simple French toast. I like to top mine with some warm apple compote or fresh maple syrup I picked up at my local farmers' market.

Serves 8

1 loaf French bread, cubed
6 eggs
2 c. milk
1-1/2 t. cinnamon, divided
1/4 c. butter, softened
1/2 c. brown sugar, packed
1/2 c. chopped pecans
1/8 t. nutmeg

Place bread cubes in a large bowl. In a separate bowl, beat together eggs, milk and 1/2 teaspoon cinnamon. Pour egg mixture over bread; mix well. Cover and refrigerate for at least 4 hours to overnight. Spoon bread mixture into a lightly greased slow cooker. In a small bowl, mix together butter, brown sugar, pecans, remaining cinnamon and nutmeg; sprinkle over bread mixture. Cover and cook on low setting for 4 hours, or on high setting for 2 hours. Let stand 15 to 20 minutes before serving.

Jen Thomas, *Santa Rosa, CA*

Viennese Coffee

Stir up this flavorful coffee in the crock for your next brunch.

Serves 6 to 8

6 c. hot brewed coffee
6 T. chocolate syrup
2 t. sugar
2/3 c. whipping cream
Optional: 1/2 c. creme de cacao or Irish
   creme liqueur
Garnish: whipped cream, chocolate shavings
   or sprinkles

Combine coffee, chocolate syrup and sugar in a slow cooker. Cover and cook on low setting for 2 to 2-1/2 hours. Stir in cream and liqueur, if using. Cover and cook an additional 30 minutes, or until heated through. Serve coffee in mugs, topped with dollops of whipped cream and garnished as desired.

Lynda Robson, *Boston, MA*

Mrs. Finnegan's Pumpkin Tea Bread

A good family friend of ours used to make this bread all the time. She'd give us loaves wrapped in colorful plastic wrap tied with a big bow. We couldn't wait to slice it up and dig in!

Makes one loaf

1/2 c. oil
1/2 c. sugar

1/2 c. brown sugar, packed
2 eggs, beaten
1 c. canned pumpkin
1-1/2 c. all-purpose flour
3/4 t. salt
1/2 t. cinnamon
1/2 t. nutmeg
1 t. baking soda

In a bowl, mix together oil and sugars. Stir in eggs and pumpkin; set aside. In a separate bowl, mix together flour, salt, cinnamon, nutmeg and baking soda. Stir flour mixture into pumpkin mixture until combined. Spoon batter into a greased 32-ounce metal coffee can; place in slow cooker and cover with 6 to 8 paper towels. Cover and cook on high setting for 3 to 3-1/2 hours, until a toothpick tests clean.

Elizabeth Blackstone, *Racine, WI*

Berry Bog Oatmeal

Cranberries and a touch of honey turn ordinary oatmeal into breakfast the whole family looks forward to.

Serves 4

1 c. steel-cut oats, uncooked
1 c. sweetened dried cranberries
1 c. chopped dates
4 c. water
1/2 c. half-and-half
2 T. honey

Combine oats, cranberries, dates and water in a greased slow cooker. Cover and cook on low setting for 6 to 8 hours. Stir in half-and-half and honey.

Berry Bog Oatmeal

Parmesan Biscuit Bread

Vickie, *Gooseberry Patch*

Parmesan Biscuit Bread

Nothing says comfort like warm, fresh-baked bread...and what could be easier than putting your slow cooker to work "baking" it for you?

Makes one loaf

1-1/2 c. biscuit baking mix
2 egg whites, beaten
1/2 c. milk
1 T. dried, minced onion
1 T. sugar
1-1/2 t. garlic powder
1/4 c. grated Parmesan cheese

Combine all ingredients except Parmesan cheese; stir well. Lightly grease a 2-1/2 to 3-quart slow cooker; spoon dough into slow cooker and sprinkle with cheese. Cover and cook on high setting one to 1-1/4 hours. Remove from slow cooker and cut into wedges to serve.

Marlene Burns, *Swisher, IA*

Hot Vanilla Treat

This beverage is perfect for a chilly fall night. Sometimes I even use it as a coffee creamer.

Serves 8

1/2 gal. milk
2 4-inch cinnamon sticks
3 T. sugar
2 T. vanilla extract
1/8 t. salt

1/8 t. nutmeg
Garnish: whipped cream, cinnamon

Combine all ingredients except garnish in a slow cooker; mix well to dissolve sugar. Cover and cook on low setting for 2 to 3 hours, until hot. Garnish servings with whipped cream and a sprinkle of cinnamon.

Lisa Ragland, *Columbus, OH*

Zucchini-Walnut Bread

With this tasty recipe, there's no such thing as too many zucchini!

Makes one loaf

2 eggs
2/3 c. oil
1-1/4 c. sugar
2 t. vanilla extract
1-1/3 c. zucchini, peeled and shredded
2 c. all-purpose flour
1 t. cinnamon
1/2 t. baking powder
1/2 t. nutmeg
1/4 t. salt
1/2 to 1 c. chopped walnuts

Beat eggs until light and foamy in a mixing bowl with an electric mixer at high speed. Add oil, sugar, vanilla and zucchini; mix well and set aside. Mix remaining ingredients in another bowl; add to egg mixture and mix well. Pour into a greased and floured 2-pound metal coffee can or a 2-quart mold. Cover top with 8 paper towels to absorb condensation; set in a slow cooker. Cover and cook on high setting for 3 to 4 hours. Let stand 5 minutes before unmolding.

Patricia Coulter, *Canmer, KY*

Mock Apple Butter

An Amish friend shared this recipe with me after hearing me comment about the abundance of zucchini we had last summer.

Makes about 5 pints

8 c. zucchini, peeled, seeded and diced
12-oz. can frozen apple juice concentrate
1 c. sugar
1 t. cinnamon
1/2 c. red cinnamon candies
5 1-pint canning jars and lids, sterilized

Combine all ingredients in a slow cooker; mix well. Cover and cook on low setting for 8 to 10 hours. Transfer mixture to a blender or food processor; purée until smooth. Ladle hot mixture into hot sterilized jars, leaving 1/2-inch headspace. Wipe rims; secure with lids and rings. Process in a boiling water bath for 10 minutes. Set jars on a towel to cool; check for seals.

Connie Hilty, *Pearland, TX*

Creamy Banana French Toast

Full of amazing flavors, this French toast is loaded with bananas and it's baked in the slow cooker.

Serves 6

10-inch loaf day-old French baguette, cut into
    1-inch slices
1/2 c. cream cheese, room temperature
3 to 4 bananas, sliced into rounds
2 T. light brown sugar, packed
1/2 c. chopped walnuts or pecans
2 T. butter, thinly sliced
3 eggs, beaten
1/4 c. milk
1/3 c. honey
1-1/2 t. vanilla extract
1 t. cinnamon
1/8 t. nutmeg
Garnish: additional honey

Lightly grease a 6-1/2 quart slow cooker with non-stick vegetable spray; set aside. Spread both sides of bread slices with cream cheese. Arrange bread in a single layer in the bottom of slow cooker. Layer banana slices over bread; sprinkle with brown sugar and nuts. Dot with butter; set aside. In a bowl, whisk together eggs, milk, honey, vanilla and spices until well blended. Pour egg mixture over bread; it should cover bread about 3/4 of the way. If not, add a little more milk. Cover and cook on low setting for 3 to 4 hours, or on high setting for 2 to 2-1/2 hours. Uncover; if not serving immediately, turn to warm setting. Transfer to plates; drizzle with honey and serve.

Creamy Banana French Toast

Pumpkin Spice Latte

Marsha Baker, *Pioneer, OH*

Pumpkin Spice Latte

Why go out and pay for a similar latte when you can make one just as tasty in your own kitchen? This drink is delicious, and it makes the house smell delicious too!

Serves 2 to 3

2 c. milk
1/2 c. brewed espresso, or 3/4 c. strong
   brewed coffee
2 T. canned pumpkin
2 T. sugar
2 T. vanilla extract
1/2 t. pumpkin pie spice
Garnish: whipped cream, cinnamon

Combine milk and espresso or coffee in a mini slow cooker. Whisk in pumpkin, sugar, vanilla and spice until combined. Cover and cook on high setting for 2 hours, or until warmed through. Whisk again before serving. Top mugs with a dollop of whipped cream and sprinkle with cinnamon.

Julianne Saifullah, *Lexington, KY*

Shamrock Breakfast Bake

This overnight Southwestern-inspired breakfast bake, studded with green, is a fun way to greet the morning on St. Patrick's Day. This recipe can be doubled for a larger gathering...why not surprise your co-workers? They'll certainly feel lucky!

Serves 4 to 5

1/2 lb. ground pork breakfast sausage, browned
   and crumbled
4-oz. can diced green chiles, drained
1/2 onion, diced
1/2 green pepper, diced
1-1/2 c. shredded Monterey Jack cheese
10 eggs, beaten

Spray a slow cooker with non-stick vegetable spray. Add 1/3 of sausage to slow cooker; top with 1/3 each of chiles, onion, pepper and cheese. Repeat layers, ending with a layer of cheese. Pour eggs over top. Cover and cook on low setting for 7 to 8 hours, until cooked through.

~ *Handy Tip* ~
A super-easy fresh breakfast side dish...fruit kabobs! Just slide strawberries, melon cubes, pineapple chunks and grapes onto wooden skewers.

Chapter Five

Simple Sweet
Snacks
& Desserts

Let us count the ways! So sweet are slow-cooker desserts. We love them and since we can just toss most of the ingredients in and walk away, it seems they love us back! Hot Fudge Turtle Brownies are sure to fill your tummy with joy. Summer Berry Cobbler has your picnic plans all set! It's easy and delicious...just right for a summer evening under the stars. Gingerbread Pudding Cake makes holiday time simple and is a special recipe for making memories with loved ones. You'll find slow-cooker desserts everyone will love for every occasion!

Jo Ann, *Gooseberry Patch*

Bananas Foster

Be sure your bananas are ripe but not too soft...otherwise they'll turn into mush in the slow cooker.

Serves 4

1/2 c. butter, melted
1/4 c. brown sugar, packed
6 bananas, cut into one-inch slices
1/4 c. rum or 1/4 t. rum extract
Garnish: vanilla ice cream

Stir together butter, brown sugar, bananas and rum or extract in a 3-quart slow cooker. Cover and cook on low setting for one hour. To serve, spoon over scoops of vanilla ice cream.

Leisha Howard, *Seattle, WA*

Slow-Cooker Tapioca Pudding

A sweet traditional recipe.

Serves 10 to 12

8 c. milk
1 c. small pearl tapioca, uncooked
1 to 1-1/2 c. sugar
4 eggs, beaten
1 t. vanilla extract
1/2 t. almond extract
Garnish: whipped cream, sliced fresh fruit

Add milk, tapioca and sugar to a slow cooker; stir gently. Cover and cook on high setting for 3 hours. Mix together eggs, extracts and 2 spoonfuls of hot mixture from slow cooker in a bowl. Slowly stir mixture into slow cooker. Cover and cook on high setting for an additional 20 minutes. Chill overnight. Garnish as desired.

Graceann Frederico, *Irondequoit, NY*

Favorite Caramel Apples

Press candy-coated chocolates, candy corn, red cinnamon candies or chocolate chips into the warm caramel for a special treat.

Makes 8.

2 14-oz. pkgs. caramels, unwrapped
1/4 c. water
1/2 t. cinnamon
8 wooden skewers
8 apples
Optional: chopped nuts

Combine caramels, water and cinnamon in a slow cooker. Cover and cook on high setting for one to 1-1/2 hours, stirring frequently. Insert sticks into apples. Reduce heat to low setting. Dip apples into hot caramel and turn to coat, scraping excess caramel from bottom of apples. Roll in chopped nuts, if desired. Place on greased wax paper to cool.

Favorite Caramel Apples

Megan Brooks, *Antioch, TN*

Apple-Cranberry Dessert

A sweet fruity dessert.

Serves 6

6 apples, peeled, cored and sliced
1 c. cranberries
1 c. sugar
1/2 t. orange zest
1/2 c. water
3 T. port wine or orange juice
Optional: whipping cream, orange zest

Arrange apples and cranberries in a lightly greased slow cooker; sprinkle with sugar. Add orange zest, water and wine or juice. Stir to mix. Cover and cook on low setting for 4 to 6 hours, until apples are tender. Spoon into serving bowls; pour whipping cream over top and garnish with orange zest, if desired.

Susan Bick, *Ballwin, MO*

Easy Blueberry Dessert

Just as delicious if you substitute cherry or apple pie filling!

Serves 10 to 12

21-oz. can blueberry pie filling
18-1/2 oz. pkg. yellow cake mix
1/2 c. butter, melted
1/3 c. chopped walnuts
Garnish: vanilla ice cream

Place pie filling in a lightly greased slow cooker. In a bowl, combine dry cake mix and butter. Mixture will be crumbly. Sprinkle over pie filling. Sprinkle with walnuts. Cover and cook on low setting for 4 hours, or on high setting for 2 hours. Allow to cool slightly. To serve, scoop into bowls and top with ice cream.

Samantha Sparks, *Madison, WI*

Mom's Rice Porridge

You can also use medium-grain or short-grain rice in this recipe.

Serves 2 to 4

1 c. long-cooking rice, uncooked
2 c. water
12-oz. can evaporated milk
1/2 c. raisins
1/2 t. salt
Garnish: cinnamon

Combine all ingredients except garnish in a slow cooker. Cover and cook on low setting for 6 to 8 hours, or overnight. Garnish with cinnamon.

~ *Time Saver* ~

Cut cleanup time in half by using slow cooker liners.

Slow-Cooker Caramel Apple Pie Dip

Amy Butcher, Columbus, GA

Slow-Cooker Caramel Apple Pie Dip

A great recipe to build tradition and fond memories...it's special, delicious and festive!

Serves 8

5 c. apples, peeled, cored and diced
12-1/4 oz. jar caramel ice cream topping
1/2 t. cinnamon
1/8 t. nutmeg
1/8 t. salt
1 T. cornstarch
2 T. cold water

In a 4-quart slow cooker, combine apples, caramel topping, spices and salt; set aside. In a cup, mix together cornstarch and water; add to mixture in slow cooker. Stir gently until well mixed. Cover and cook on high setting for 2 hours, stirring once or twice while cooking. Serve dip warm with Crust Dippers.

Crust Dippers:

1/2 t. cinnamon
2 T. sugar
2 9-inch pie crusts
2 T. milk

Combine cinnamon and sugar in a cup; set aside. Spread out each pie crust onto a lightly greased baking sheet. Brush each crust with half of milk; sprinkle with half of cinnamon-sugar. With a pizza cutter or knife, cut crusts into 2-inch by one-inch strips. Spread out strips on baking sheets, allowing some space in between strips. Bake at 350 degrees for 10 minutes, or until crisp and golden.

Sandra Sullivan, Aurora, CO

Cranberry Bread Pudding

This is the ultimate comfort food. It's a favorite fall recipe for when time is short and the oven is full. You can substitute half-and-half for the whole milk or add chopped dried apples or other dried fruits for a tasty twist.

Serves 8

4 c. whole milk
4 eggs
1 c. sugar
2 t. vanilla extract
1/2 t. salt
Optional: 2 T. brandy
6 c. white bread cubes, toasted
1-1/2 c. sweetened dried cranberries
Garnish: powdered sugar, whipped topping

In a bowl, beat milk, eggs, sugar, vanilla, salt and brandy, if using. Place bread cubes and cranberries in a large slow cooker; drizzle egg mixture over bread mixture. Stir to coat evenly. Cover and cook on low setting for about 3-1/2 hours, just until pudding is set. Sprinkle servings with powdered sugar and top with a dollop of whipped topping.

Darcy Ericksen, *Independence, MO*

Chocolate Pudding Cake

This is such an easy treat to whip up...and I almost always have the ingredients on hand.

Makes 8 to 12 servings

3 c. milk
3.4-oz. pkg. cook & serve chocolate pudding mix
18-1/2 oz. pkg. chocolate cake mix
Garnish: frozen whipped topping, thawed

In a bowl, whisk together milk and dry pudding mix. Pour into a slow cooker that has been sprayed with non-stick vegetable spray; set aside. Prepare cake mix according to package directions; carefully pour batter into slow cooker. Do not stir. Cover and cook on high setting for 2-1/2 hours, or until cake is set. Serve warm with whipped topping.

Carol McMillion, *Catawba, VA*

Fudgy Pudding Cake

Super moist and so good topped with ice cream.

Serves 8 to 10

18-1/2 oz. pkg. chocolate cake mix
3.9-oz. pkg. instant chocolate pudding mix
16-oz. container sour cream
3/4 c. oil
4 eggs

1 c. water
6-oz. pkg. semi-sweet chocolate chips
Garnish: vanilla ice cream

Mix together all ingredients except ice cream in a large bowl. Pour into a slow cooker that has been sprayed with non-stick vegetable spray. Cover and cook on low setting for 6 to 8 hours. Turn off slow cooker and let stand 20 to 30 minutes; do not lift lid until ready to serve. Serve with vanilla ice cream.

Sharon Jones, *Oklahoma City, OK*

Cinnamon Streusel Cake

A delightful brunch treat, too.

Serves 10

16-oz. pkg. pound cake mix
1/4 c. brown sugar, packed
1 T. all-purpose flour
1 t. cinnamon
1/4 c. nuts, finely chopped
Garnish: ice cream

Prepare cake mix batter according to package directions. Pour into a generously greased and floured 2-pound metal coffee can. Mix brown sugar, flour, cinnamon and nuts in a small bowl; sprinkle over batter. Cover can with 6 to 8 paper towels to absorb condensation; place in a slow cooker. Cover and cook on high setting for 3 to 4 hours. Serve with a scoop of ice cream.

Cinnamon Streusel Cake

Emily Martin, *Ontario, Canada*

Warm Fruited Pudding

Use your slow cooker to slowly steam this deliciously moist pudding. Displayed on a cake stand, it adds a pretty, festive touch to your holiday buffet!

Serves 16

3/4 c. butter, softened
3/4 c. sugar
2 eggs
1/2 c. orange or apple juice
1 c. all-purpose flour
3/4 t. baking powder
1/2 t. baking soda
1 t. salt
1 t. cinnamon
1/2 t. allspice
1 c. dry bread crumbs
2 c. raisins
1-1/2 c. mixed candied fruit, chopped

In a large bowl, beat butter and sugar until fluffy. Beat in eggs, one at a time; stir in juice. In a separate bowl, combine remaining ingredients; mix well. Gradually add butter mixture to flour mixture; stir until moistened. Pour into a greased 8-cup pudding mold. Cover with greased aluminum foil. Place on a rack in a large slow cooker. Pour boiling water into slow cooker; fill to halfway up the sides of pudding pan. Cover and cook on high setting for 4 hours. Carefully remove pudding mold from slow cooker; invert onto a serving plate.

Donna Fisher, *Delaware, OH*

Razzleberry Upside-Down Cake

The name may make you giggle, but this cake is so delicious that it will soon be a family favorite. You can just spoon it right out of the slow cooker.

Serves 10 to 12

3 egg whites
1-1/4 c. water
1/3 c. applesauce
0.3-oz. pkg. sugar-free raspberry gelatin mix
18-1/4 oz. pkg. cherry chip cake mix
12-oz. can red raspberry pastry filling
Garnish: fresh raspberries; frozen whipped topping, thawed

Beat egg whites in a large bowl with an electric mixer at high speed for one to 2 minutes, until soft peaks form. Add water, applesauce, gelatin mix and cake mix; beat at medium speed for 2 minutes. Spread raspberry filling into a slow cooker that has been sprayed with non-stick vegetable spray; pour cake batter mixture over top. Do not stir. Cover with 8 paper towels. Cover and cook on high setting for 2 hours. Remove crock from slow cooker; let cool for 15 minutes. Place a large rimmed serving plate on top of slow cooker. Carefully invert cake onto plate. Garnish with fresh raspberries and a dollop of whipped topping.

Razzleberry Upside-Down Cake

Vickie, *Gooseberry Patch*

Banana Pudding Cake

My family is happy when I mix up this favorite recipe and get the slow cooker going.

Serves 12

3 egg whites
1 c. bananas, mashed
18-1/2 oz. pkg. yellow cake mix
2-1/2 c. water, divided
3-oz. pkg. cook & serve banana pudding mix

Beat egg whites with an electric mixer at high speed until soft peaks form, about one to 2 minutes. Beat bananas in a separate bowl until puréed; add to egg whites. Add dry cake mix and 1/2 cup water; beat for one to 2 minutes. Set aside. Spray a slow cooker with non-stick vegetable spray. Combine remaining water and dry pudding mix in a small bowl, stirring until dissolved. Add pudding mixture to cake batter; beat for one minute or until combined. Pour mixture into slow cooker; do not stir. Place 8 paper towels on top to absorb moisture. Cover and cook on high setting for 2 hours. Uncover slow cooker; place a large rimmed serving plate on top of slow cooker. Carefully invert cake onto plate.

Audrey Lett, *Newark, DE*

Hot Fudge Turtle Brownies

What makes people smile more than yummy chocolate fudge brownies?

Serves 10

18.4-oz. pkg. fudge brownie mix
2/3 c. mini semi-sweet chocolate chips
2/3 c. oil
2 eggs, beaten
1/4 c. water
11-oz. pkg. caramel baking bits
1/3 c. whipping cream
3/4 c. chopped pecans
12-oz. jar hot fudge sauce
3/4 c. hot water

In a large bowl, combine dry brownie mix, chocolate chips, oil, eggs and water. Whisk together just until combined; do not overmix. Pour batter into a greased 6-quart slow cooker; set aside. In a microwave-safe bowl, combine caramel chips and cream. Microwave on high setting, stirring after every 30 seconds, until caramel is completely melted. Stir in pecans. Pour caramel mixture over brownie mixture; use a knife to swirl in caramel. In a small bowl, whisk together hot fudge sauce and hot water until smooth. Drizzle over caramel mixture. Cover and cook on high setting for 3 to 3-1/2 hours, until brownies are set around the edges.

Hot Fudge Turtle Brownies

Toffee Fondue

Michelle Riihl, *Windom, MN*

Toffee Fondue

Just perfect for sharing with girlfriends! Try dipping pretzel twists too...the salty-sweet combo is delectable.

Serves 10

14-oz. pkg. caramels, unwrapped
1/4 c. milk
1/4 c. strong black coffee
1/2 c. milk chocolate chips
apple wedges, banana chunks, marshmallows,
   angel food cake cubes

Mix together caramels, milk, coffee and chocolate chips in a small slow cooker. Cover and cook on low setting until melted, 2 to 3 hours. Stir well. Serve with fruit, marshmallows and cake cubes for dipping.

～ *Handy Tip* ～

Prefer not to leave the slow cooker on while you're away? Simple...put it to work overnight! In the morning, refrigerate food in a fridge container... reheat at suppertime.

Jo Ann, *Gooseberry Patch*

Summer Berry Cobbler

Serve warm topped with whipped cream or ice cream...a delectable summer dessert best enjoyed on the front porch at the day's end, listening to a chorus of crickets for entertainment.

Serves 8 to 10

5 c. mixed berries, such as raspberries,
   blueberries, blackberries or strawberries
1 c. sugar, divided
2-3/4 c. biscuit baking mix, divided
1/4 c. butter, melted
1/2 c. milk
2 t. cinnamon

Spray a slow cooker with non-stick vegetable spray. In a large bowl, toss together berries, 1/2 cup sugar and 1/2 cup baking mix. Transfer mixture to slow cooker. In another bowl, stir together remaining baking mix, 1/4 cup remaining sugar, melted butter and milk until a soft dough forms. Using your hands, drop dollops of dough on top of berries in the slow cooker. In a small bowl, stir together remaining sugar and cinnamon; sprinkle over dough. Do not stir. Cover and cook on high setting for 2 to 2-1/2 hours, until dough is puffy and fruit is bubbly.

Paula Marchesi, *Lenhartsville, PA*

Apple-Peanut Crumble

Everyone in my house loves dessert, and this crumble is quick & easy to fix. Just set it in the slow cooker, leave it, then serve! I enjoy making it in the fall, but it's scrumptious year 'round.

Serves 4 to 5

4 to 5 Granny Smith apples, peeled, cored and
    sliced
2/3 c. brown sugar, packed
1/2 c. all-purpose flour
1/2 c. quick-cooking oats, uncooked
1/2 t. cinnamon
1/4 t. to 1/2 t. nutmeg
1/3 c. butter, softened
2 T. crunchy peanut butter
Garnish: vanilla ice cream, cocktail peanuts

Place apple slices in a lightly greased slow cooker; set aside. In a bowl, combine brown sugar, flour, oats and spices. Cut in butter and peanut butter with a pastry blender or 2 forks until mixture is crumbly. Sprinkle sugar mixture over apples. Cover and cook on low setting for 5 to 6 hours. Serve crumble in bowls, topped with a scoop of ice cream and a sprinkling of peanuts.

Jo Ann, *Gooseberry Patch*

Raisin Bread Pudding in Vanilla Sauce

A slow-cooker version of a classic dessert.

Serves 6

8 slices bread, cubed
4 eggs
2 c. milk
1/2 c. sugar
1/4. c. butter, melted
1/4 c. raisins
1/2 t. cinnamon

Place bread cubes in a greased slow cooker and set aside. Whisk together eggs and milk in a bowl; stir in remaining ingredients. Pour over bread cubes and stir. Cover and cook on high setting for one hour. Reduce setting to low; cook an additional 3 to 4 hours. Serve warm with Vanilla Sauce.

Vanilla Sauce:

2 T. butter
2 T. all-purpose flour
1 c. water
3/4 c. sugar
1 t. vanilla extract

Melt butter in a small saucepan over medium heat; stir in flour until smooth. Gradually add water, sugar and vanilla. Bring to a boil; cook and stir 2 minutes, or until thickened. Keep warm.

Raisin Bread Pudding in Vanilla Sauce

Vickie, *Gooseberry Patch*

Coconut-Mango Rice Pudding

A delectably different dessert for your springtime gathering.

Makes 8 to 10 servings

1 c. long-cooking white rice, uncooked
1-1/2 t. cinnamon
4 slices fresh ginger, peeled and diced
15-oz. can coconut milk
4 c. milk
1 c. sugar
2 t. vanilla extract
2 T. sesame seed
1 mango, peeled and diced
honey to taste

Place rice, cinnamon and ginger in a slow cooker. In a bowl, whisk together milks, sugar and vanilla. Pour over rice. Cover and cook on high setting for 3 to 3 -1/2 hours, stirring once or twice, until rice is fully cooked and milk is absorbed. Just before serving, toast sesame seed in a dry skillet over medium heat until just golden. Serve individual portions of rice pudding topped with diced mango, honey and sesame seed.

Annette Ingram, *Grand Rapids, MI*

Pumpkin Pie Dump Cake

This fall favorite is so easy to make. I can keep the kids busy with helping add the ingredients to the crock.

Serves 6

2 15-oz. cans pumpkin
1/2 c. sugar
2 t. pumpkin pie spice
1/2 t. salt
15-1/4 oz. pkg. white or yellow cake mix
1/2 c. butter, melted
1/2 c. chopped pecans
Garnish: whipped cream

In a large bowl, stir together pumpkin, sugar, spice and salt. Pour into a lightly greased 6-quart slow cooker. Sprinkle dry cake mix over top. Drizzle evenly with melted butter; sprinkle with pecans. Cover and cook on low setting for 4 to 4-1/2 hours, until set. Serve warm, topped with a dollop of whipped cream.

Pumpkin Dump Cake

Monkey Bread

Cathy Hillier, *Salt Lake City, UT*

Monkey Bread

A sweet and delicious bread that can be served up any day of the week.

Serves 14

1/4 c. very warm water, 105 to 115 degrees
1/4 c. sugar, divided
2-1/2 t. instant yeast
5 c. all-purpose flour
1 t. salt
1-1/4 c. very warm milk, 105 to 115 degrees
1/4 c. butter, melted and divided
2 eggs, lightly beaten

In a small bowl, combine warm water and one tablespoon sugar; stir in yeast. Set aside for 5 minutes, until yeast has dissolved and mixture begins to foam. Meanwhile, in a large bowl, stir together 2 cups flour, remaining sugar and salt. Add yeast mixture, warm milk, melted butter and eggs to flour mixture. Beat with an electric mixer on low speed until combined. Add remaining flour; beat on low speed until a soft but not sticky dough forms. Turn dough out onto a lightly floured surface; let stand for 10 minutes. Meanwhile, prepare Coatings. Shape dough into balls by 2-tablespoon portions. Roll each ball in melted butter, then in sugar mixture to coat evenly. Grease the bottom of a 7-quart slow cooker; arrange balls in slow cooker. Place 2 paper towels over top of slow cooker, to prevent condensation. Cover and cook on high setting for 2 hours, or until set. Turn bread out onto a large serving plate; serve warm.

Coatings:

3/4 c. butter
1 c. sugar
3/4 c. light brown sugar, packed
2 t. cinnamon

Melt butter in a small bowl. In a separate bowl, combine the sugars and cinnamon. Set aside.

Mel Chencharick, *Julian, PA*

Black Forest Cake-Cobbler

When I was given this recipe to try, I didn't believe you could make a cake in a slow cooker. Well, yes you can! It's not exactly a cake, and not quite a cobbler..but it's scrumptious! It combines the taste of chocolate and cherry. A big "thank you" to Christie for this terrific recipe.

Makes 10 servings

1/2 c. butter, melted
8-oz. can crushed pineapple, drained and juice reserved
21-oz. can cherry pie filling
18-1/4 oz. pkg. chocolate cake mix
Garnish: whipped topping

In a bowl, mix melted butter with reserved pineapple juice; set aside. Spread crushed pineapple evenly in the bottom of a slow cooker. Spoon pie filling evenly over pineapple. Sprinkle dry cake mix over pie filling. Stir butter mixture again; drizzle over cake mix. Cover and cook on low setting for 3 hours. To serve, spoon into dessert bowls; let cool about 5 minutes, as pie filling will be very hot. Garnish with a dollop of whipped topping.

Rogene Rogers, *Bemidji, MN*

Lemon-Poppy Seed Cake

This cake is so light and refreshing!

Serves 10 to 12

15.8-oz. lemon-poppy seed bread mix
1 egg, beaten
8-oz. container sour cream
1-1/4 c. water, divided
1/2 c. sugar
1/4 c. lemon juice
1 T. butter

Combine bread mix, egg, sour cream and 1/2 cup water in a bowl. Stir until well moistened; spread in a lightly greased 3 to 4-quart slow cooker. Combine 3/4 cup water and remaining ingredients in a small saucepan; bring to a boil. Pour boiling mixture over batter in slow cooker. Cover and cook on high setting for 2 to 2-1/2 hours, until edges are

golden. Turn off slow cooker; let cake cool in slow cooker for 30 minutes with lid ajar. When cool enough to handle, hold a large plate over top of slow cooker and invert to turn out cake.

Ellie Brandel, *Clackamas, OR*

Chocolate-Nut Pudding

This pudding is delicious! Gooey chocolate and chopped nuts are a perfect combination. Change up the flavor and top this dessert with some caramel or chocolate ice cream instead of vanilla.

Serves 4 to 6

1-1/2 c. biscuit baking mix
1 c. sugar, divided
1/2 c. milk
1 egg, beaten
2 T. oil
1 t. vanilla extract
1/2 c. chopped nuts
6-oz. pkg. semi-sweet chocolate chips, melted
1-1/2 c. hot water
Garnish: vanilla ice cream or whipped topping

In a large bowl, beat together baking mix, 1/3 cup sugar, milk, egg, oil and vanilla until smooth. Stir in nuts and melted chocolate. Spoon batter into a lightly greased slow cooker. In a bowl, stir together remaining sugar and water until sugar is dissolved; drizzle over batter. Cover and cook on low setting for 8 to 10 hours. Serve pudding topped with a scoop of ice cream or a dollop of whipped topping.

Kay Marone, *Des Moines, IA*

New York Style Cheesecake

A special recipe for a special occasion.

Serves 6

3/4 c. graham cracker crumbs
1 T. butter, melted
1/2 c. plus 1 T. sugar, divided
1/2 t. salt, divided
2 8-oz. pkgs. cream cheese, softened
2 eggs
1/3 c. sour cream
1 t. all-purpose flour
1 t. vanilla extract

Pour one inch of water into a 6-quart slow cooker. Crumble aluminum foil and place inside slow cooker as a rack; set aside. Grease a 6" springform pan; wrap tightly with 2 layers of foil. In a large bowl, stir together graham cracker crumbs, butter, one tablespoon sugar and 1/4 teaspoon salt. Press crumb mixture into greased pan, forming a crust; add to slow cooker and set aside. In a large bowl, with an electric mixer on medium speed, beat cream cheese and remaining 1/2 cup sugar until fluffy. Add eggs, sour cream, flour, vanilla and remaining salt; beat until combined. Pour cream cheese mixture into crust. Top slow cooker with 3 layers of paper towels to catch any condensation. Cover and cook on high setting for 2 hours. Turn off slow cooker; let stand for one hour. Carefully remove cheesecake in pan from slow cooker; remove foil from pan. Refrigerate at least 4 hours to overnight, until completely chilled.

Lori Rosenburg, *University Heights, OH*

Crispy Rice Treats

This recipe yields the same great results as the traditional method of making crispy rice bars, but with a lot less mess in the kitchen, which makes it a winner in my book!

Serves 12

3 T. butter, sliced
4 c. mini marshmallows
6 c. crispy rice cereal

Place butter in a slow cooker; add marshmallows and cereal. Cover and cook on high setting for one hour. Stir well. If needed, cover and cook for 15 to 20 minutes longer, until marshmallows are fully melted. Butter an 11"x9" glass baking pan. Transfer mixture from slow cooker to baking pan; press mixture firmly into pan, using a buttered spatula or your hands. Cool; cut into squares.

Pumpkin Streusel Coffee Cake

John Alexander, New Britain, CT

Pumpkin Streusel Coffee Cake

This breakfast cake is pure comfort food! Moist and tender pumpkin cake topped with a thick cinnamon oat streusel...you won't have any leftovers! But if you do, store them wrapped in foil or plastic wrap in the refrigerator for up to 4 days.

Serves 12

2 c. whole-wheat pastry flour
1-1/2 t. baking powder
1/2 t. baking soda
1-1/2 t. cinnamon
1/4 t. nutmeg
1/4 t. ginger
1/4 t. salt
1 T. butter, melted and cooled slightly
1 egg white
1 t. vanilla extract
1 c. canned pumpkin
1 t. lemon juice or vinegar
1/3 c. maple syrup

Line a 5-quart slow cooker with aluminum foil; spray lightly with non-stick vegetable spray and set aside. In a bowl, combine flour, baking powder, baking soda, spices and salt; mix well and set aside. In a separate large bowl, combine butter, egg white and vanilla. Stir in pumpkin, lemon juice and maple syrup. Gradually add flour mixture to pumpkin mixture; stir just until mixed. Spread batter in slow cooker. Sprinkle evenly with Crumb Topping, pressing topping lightly into batter. Cover cook on low setting for 2 hours and 15 minutes. Turn off slow cooker. Let coffee cake cool in crock for 10 minutes; remove, using the edges of the foil as handles. Set on a wire rack; cool to room temperature before serving.

Crumb Topping:

1 c. brown sugar, packed
1 c. all-purpose flour
1-1/4 t. cinnamon
2 t. butter, softened

Combine brown sugar, flour, cinnamon and butter; mix well.

Jessica Zelkovich, Hamilton, IL

Easy-Peasy Berry Cobbler

You'll love this super-simple and delicious dessert...there's only four ingredients!

Serves 6 to 8

16-oz. pkg. frozen mixed berries
1/2 c. sugar
12-oz. tube refrigerated biscuits
cinnamon to taste

Pour frozen berries into a slow cooker; stir in sugar. Arrange biscuits on top; sprinkle with cinnamon. Cover and cook on high setting for 3 hours. Serve warm.

Terri Kearney, *Maple Hill, NC*

Cinnamon-Raisin Bread

My husband, my best friend and my mother-in-law can all agree on on one thing...they love this warm and hearty bread pudding!

Makes 8 servings

4 c. cinnamon-raisin bread, toasted and cubed
2 eggs
3/4 c. sugar
2-1/2 c. milk, heated to boiling and cooled
2 T. butter, melted
1 t. vanilla extract
1/8 t. nutmeg
1/8 t. salt
Garnish: whipped cream

Add bread cubes to a slow cooker that has been sprayed with non-stick vegetable spray. In a bowl, beat eggs and sugar; whisk in remaining ingredients except garnish. Pour over bread cubes, mixing well and pressing down so bread will soak up milk mixture. Cover and cook on low setting for 6 hours. Spoon into individual bowls; serve warm topped with whipped cream.

Beth Kramer, *Port Saint Lucie, FL*

Autumn Brownies

This recipe of peanut butter and sweet chocolate is hard to resist...grab while you still can, they don't last long!

Serves 12

1/2 c. butter, melted
2/3 c. baking cocoa
1-1/3 c. sugar
2 eggs, beaten
1/2 t. salt
3/4 c. all-purpose flour
1 c. semi-sweet chocolate chips, divided
1/3 c. creamy peanut butter, melted

In a large bowl, stir together melted butter, cocoa and sugar until smooth. Add eggs and salt; stir until mixed well. Stir in flour; fold in 2/3 cup chocolate chips. Spread batter in a parchment paper-lined slow cooker, sprayed with non-stick vegetable spray. Drizzle melted peanut butter over batter; swirl gently with a toothpick. Sprinkle with remaining chocolate chips. Cover and cook on low setting for 2 hours. Uncover; continue cooking another 30 minutes. Lift brownies out of slow cooker, using parchment paper as handles; cool on a wire rack.

~ Gift Giving ~

Cut brownies with a round cookie cutter. Stack them inside a wide-mouthed glass jar, layered with circles of parchment paper.

Autumn Brownies

Carrot Cake

Athena Colegrove, Big Springs, TX

Carrot Cake

Mom made this recipe...it's a childhood favorite!

Serves 8

1-1/4 c. unsweetened applesauce
2 c. sugar
3 eggs, room temperature
2 c. all-purpose flour
1-1/2 t. baking powder
1 t. baking soda
1 t. cinnamon
1 t. salt
2 c. carrots, peeled and grated
1 c. sweetened shredded coconut
8-1/4 oz. can crushed pineapple
1 t. vanilla extract

Line the inside of a medium slow cooker with aluminum foil, forming "handles" up over the top. Place a slow-cooker liner into foil-lined crock; spray with non-stick cooking spray and set aside. In a large bowl, whisk together applesauce, sugar and eggs. Add flour, baking powder, baking soda, salt and cinnamon; mix well. Stir in carrots, coconut, pineapple with juice and vanilla. Pour batter into slow cooker. Place several paper towels on top of slow cooker to absorb any condensation. Cover and cook on low setting for 2 hours, rotating crock inside the base every 30 minutes, until a toothpick tests clean. Use the edges of the foil to remove the cake to a wire rack. Cool completely; spread with Cream Cheese Frosting.

Cream Cheese Frosting:

1/2 c. butter, softened
8-oz. pkg. cream cheese, softened
1 t. vanilla extract
1 c. powdered sugar

Beat butter and cream cheese until fluffy. Mix in vanilla and powdered sugar.

Jessica Shrout, Flintstone, MD

Jessica's Mixed Fruit Crisp

This is a wonderful dessert for family gatherings and potlucks. Everyone loves it, and it makes the whole house smell yummy!

Makes 6 to 8 servings

1 c. brown sugar, packed
1/2 c. sugar
4 Granny Smith apples, cored and cubed
2 Bosc pears, cored and cubed
1/3 c. raisins
2 t. cinnamon
1/4 t. salt
Garnish: vanilla ice cream or whipped cream

Mix sugars in a slow cooker, spreading out into an even layer. Top with apples, pears and raisins; sprinkle with cinnamon and salt. Spread Crisp Topping over all. Cover and cook on high setting for 2-1/2 hours. Turn off slow cooker; let stand, covered, for one hour before serving. Scoop crisp into dessert dishes; serve topped with ice cream or whipped cream.

Crisp Topping:

1 c. long-cooking oats, uncooked
1 c. brown sugar, packed
1/4 c. all-purpose flour
1/2 t. cinnamon
1/2 t. nutmeg
3 to 4 T. butter, cubed and softened

Mix all ingredients except butter in a bowl. Work in butter with a fork until mixture has a sandy texture.

Peanut Butter & Fudge Pudding Cake

Molly Wilson, *Rapid City, SD*

Peanut Butter & Fudge Pudding Cake

Bake a cake in a slow cooker! Kids big & little are sure to want seconds when you serve this cake warm with ice cream...yummy!

Serves 6

1/2 c. all-purpose flour
3/4 c. sugar, divided
3/4 t. baking powder
1/3 c. milk
1 T. oil
1/2 t. vanilla extract
1/4 c. creamy peanut butter
3 T. baking cocoa
1 c. boiling water

In a large bowl, combine flour, 1/4 cup sugar and baking powder. Add milk, oil and vanilla; mix until smooth. Stir in peanut butter; pour into a lightly greased slow cooker and set aside. Mix together cocoa and remaining sugar; gradually stir in boiling water. Pour mixture over batter in slow cooker; do not stir. Cover and cook on high setting 2 to 3 hours, or until a toothpick inserted in center comes out clean.

— Handy Tip —

Sour cream, milk and yogurt tend to break down in the slow cooker, so stir them in during the last 15 minutes of cooking, unless specified otherwise.

Laura Fuller, *Fort Wayne, IN*

Slow-Cooked Vanilla Custard

There's something magical about a simple, tasty vanilla custard. Can't find vanilla bean paste? Just use the same amount of pure vanilla extract instead...it'll be just as tasty.

Serves 4

12-oz. can evaporated milk
1/2 c. milk
1 t. vanilla bean paste
1 egg, lightly beaten
2 egg yolks
1/3 c. sugar

Combine milks in a saucepan over medium heat. Bring to a simmer; cook for 4 minutes. Remove from heat; whisk in vanilla bean paste. In a bowl, combine egg, egg yolks and sugar; whisk until blended. Slowly whisk milk mixture into egg mixture until smooth. Spoon custard mixture into four 8-ounce ramekins; cover tightly with aluminum foil. Place ramekins on a rack or trivet in a large slow cooker; make sure ramekins do not touch each other or sides of slow cooker. Pour hot water into slow cooker to depth of one inch up sides of ramekins. Cover and cook on high setting for 2 hours, or until a knife tip inserted in custard tests clean. Remove ramekins to a wire rack to cool. Serve warm or chilled.

Regina Wickline, *Pebble Beach, CA*

Lazy Apricot Preserves

These preserves are perfect in a gift basket, paired with a package of bagels and a cute jam spreader.

Makes about 2 pints

1 lb. dried apricots, finely chopped
1-3/4 c. sugar
3-1/2 c. water

Combine all ingredients in a medium slow cooker; stir to mix. Cover and cook on high setting for 2-1/2 hours, stirring twice. Uncover and cook for 2 hours, stirring occasionally, until thickened. Let cool; ladle into freezer containers or sterilized jars. Cover and refrigerate for up to 3 weeks, or freeze for up to 3 months.

Carrie O'Shea, *Marina Del Rey, CA*

Gingerbread Pudding Cake

Delicious, old-fashioned flavor with the modern convenience of a slow cooker.

Serves 6 to 8

1/4 c. butter, softened
1/4 c. sugar
1 egg white
1 t. vanilla extract
1/2 c. molasses
1 c. water
1-1/4 c. all-purpose flour
3/4 t. baking soda
1/4 t. salt
1/2 t. cinnamon
1/2 t. ground ginger
1/4 t. allspice
1/8 t. nutmeg
1/2 c. chopped pecans
6 T. brown sugar, packed
3/4 c. hot water
2/3 c. butter, melted
Garnish: whipped topping

In a large bowl, beat butter and sugar until light and fluffy. Beat in egg white and vanilla. In a separate small bowl, combine molasses and water. In another bowl, combine flour, baking soda, salt and spices. Gradually add flour mixture to butter mixture alternately with molasses mixture, beating well after each addition. Fold in pecans. Pour into a greased 3-quart slow cooker. Sprinkle with brown sugar. Combine hot water and butter; pour over brown sugar. Do not stir. Cover and cook on high setting for 2 to 2-1/2 hours, until a toothpick inserted near the center of cake tests clean. Turn off slow cooker; let stand for 15 minutes. Serve warm, scooped into bowls and garnished with whipped topping.

Gingerbread Pudding Cake

Cherry Delight

Kathy Grashoff, *Fort Wayne, IN*

Cherry Delight

This scrumptious warm dessert is delicious topped with vanilla ice cream or whipped cream. You can also use apple or blueberry pie filling instead of cherry!

Serves 10 to 12

21-oz. can cherry pie filling
18-1/4 oz. pkg. yellow cake mix
1/2 c. butter, melted
1/3 c. chopped walnuts

Place pie filling in a slow cooker. In a bowl, combine dry cake mix and butter. Mixture will be crumbly. Sprinkle over filling; top with walnuts. Cover and cook on low setting for 2 to 3 hours.

Cheri Maxwell, *Gulf Breeze, FL*

Warm & Gingery Pineapple

Spicy and warm...perfect on its own or even topped with crushed gingersnap cookies.

Serves 8 to 10

8 c. fresh pineapple, peeled, cored and cubed
1 c. brown sugar, packed
1 to 2 4-inch cinnamon sticks
4-inch piece fresh ginger, peeled and thinly
    sliced
Garnish: coconut ice cream

Combine all ingredients except garnish in a slow cooker; mix well. Cover and cook on high setting for 4 hours, or until pineapple is very soft. Discard cinnamon sticks. Serve pineapple mixture in bowls, topped with a scoop of ice cream.

Carol Van Rooy, *Ontario, Canada*

Pineapple Pudding

We first tried this pudding spooned over vanilla ice cream...it was so good, I started stirring it into my yogurt too!

Serves 4 to 5

20-oz. can crushed pineapple
1/4 c. water
2 eggs, beaten
2 T. cornstarch
1/2 to 3/4 c. sugar
Optional: ice cream, yogurt

Combine pineapple with juice, water, eggs, cornstarch and sugar in a slow cooker; mix well. Cover and cook on high setting for 30 minutes; reduce heat to low setting and cook for 3-1/2 hours more. Serve by itself, or spoon over ice cream or yogurt.

Emma Brown, *Saskatchewan, Canada*

Lemony Pear Delight

My family loves it when early fall rolls around so we can load up on pears at the farmers' market. We usually eat them fresh, but when we want a quick & easy but fancy dessert, this is our go-to.

Serves 6 to 8

6 pears, peeled, halved and cored
1 t. lemon zest
2 T. lemon juice
1/3 c. brown sugar, packed
1/4 t. nutmeg
1/2 c. cream cheese, softened
1/4 c. whipping cream
3 T. chopped pecans, toasted
Garnish: crushed sugar cookies

In a bowl, combine pears, lemon zest and juice; toss gently to coat pears. Sprinkle brown sugar and nutmeg over pears; stir. Spoon pear mixture into a slow cooker. Cover and cook on high setting for 1-1/2 to 2 hours, until pears are soft. Spoon pears into serving bowls. Stir cream cheese and whipping cream into juices in slow cooker. Increase heat to high setting and cook, whisking occasionally, until cream cheese is melted. Evenly spoon cream cheese mixture over pears; sprinkle with pecans and crushed sugar cookies.

Laurel Perry, *Loganville, GA*

Slow Peach Cobbler

This is a great dessert to share at potlucks! People won't believe that it was made in a slow cooker.

Serves 6 to 8

1/3 c. sugar
1/2 c. brown sugar, packed
3/4 c. biscuit baking mix
2 eggs, beaten
2 t. vanilla extract
2 t. butter, melted
3/4 c. evaporated milk
3 to 4 peaches, peeled, chopped and lightly mashed
3/4 t. cinnamon

Spray a slow cooker with non-stick vegetable spray. In a large bowl, combine sugars and baking mix. Add eggs, vanilla, butter and milk; stir well. Fold in peaches and cinnamon. Pour into slow cooker. Cover and cook on low setting for 6 to 8 hours, or on high setting for 3 to 4 hours. Serve warm.

Slow Peach Cobbler

Chocolate Raspberry Strata

Jill Ross, Pickerington, OH

Chocolate Raspberry Strata

Rich chocolate and red raspberries always make a winning combination. Save a few fresh raspberries to garnish individual servings...so elegant!

Serves 10

6 c. brioche or challah bread, cubed and divided
1-1/2 c. semi-sweet chocolate chips, divided
1/2 pt. fresh raspberries, divided
1/2 c. whipping cream
1/2 c. milk
4 eggs, beaten
1/4 c. sugar
1 t. vanilla extract

Place half of bread cubes in a slow cooker. Sprinkle with half of chocolate chips and raspberries. Repeat layering. In a bowl, whisk together remaining ingredients; pour over top. Cover and cook on high setting for 1-1/2 to 2 hours.

Marlene Burns, Swisher, IA

Eggnog-Gingersnap Custard

Dad loved custards, and Mom created many versions for us to try. This was one of our favorites in the fall and wintertime.

Serves 4 to 6

24 gingersnap cookies
4 eggs
1 qt. eggnog

Arrange cookies in a lightly greased slow cooker. In a bowl, beat together eggs and eggnog until well mixed; pour egg mixture over cookies. Cover and cook on low setting for 3-1/2 to 4 hours, until set. Remove crock from slow cooker and set on a wire rack to cool for 20 minutes, or chill for 4 hours.

Ann McMaster, Portland, OR

Very Berry Sauce

Got bushels of berries? Cook up some of this yummy topping. Use it to top pancakes, yogurt, ice cream...or whatever you like!

Makes 8 to 10 servings

6 c. fresh or frozen strawberries, blueberries
   or blackberries
1/2 c. sugar
2 T. quick-cooking tapioca, uncooked

Combine all ingredients in a slow cooker. Cover and cook on low setting for 4 hours, or on high setting for 2 hours, stirring occasionally.

Missie Brown, *Delaware, OH*

Upside-Down Blueberry Cake

Keep it simple...just spoon this cake out if you don't want to invert the slow cooker.

Serves 10 to 12

21-oz. can blueberry pie filling
2 eggs, separated
18-1/4 oz. pkg. lemon cake mix
1 c. water
1/3 c. applesauce

Spread pie filling in a slow cooker that has been sprayed with non-stick vegetable spray. Beat egg whites with an electric mixer at high speed until soft peaks form, about 2 minutes. Stir in egg yolks, cake mix, water and applesauce just until combined. Pour over filling; do not stir. Place 8 paper towels on top of slow cooker to absorb condensation. Cover and cook on high setting for 2 hours, or until a toothpick inserted near the center comes out clean. Remove crock from slow cooker; remove lid and paper towels. Cool cake for 15 minutes. Place a large serving plate over crock; carefully invert cake onto plate.

Tori Willis, *Champaign, IL*

Grandma's Warm Breakfast Fruit

Keep this compote warm for brunch in a mini slow cooker.

Makes about 3 cups

3 cooking apples, peeled, cored and thickly
   sliced

1 orange, peeled and sectioned
3/4 c. raisins
1/2 c. dried plums, chopped
2 bananas, sliced
8-oz. can pineapple chunks, drained

Combine all ingredients in a blender; process until blended. Transfer to a saucepan; simmer over low heat until heated through.

Dale Duncan, *Waterloo, IA*

Steamed Cranberry Pudding

A yummy bread pudding...perfect for the holidays!

Serves 8

2 T. butter, softened
2 T. sugar
1-1/3 c. all-purpose flour
1 t. baking powder
1 t. baking soda
1/2 t. salt
2 c. cranberries, halved
1/2 c. molasses
1/3 c. hot water

Butter a one-pound metal coffee can or pudding mold that will fit into your slow cooker; sprinkle with sugar and set aside. Combine flour, baking powder, baking soda and salt in a mixing bowl; stir in berries. Add molasses and hot water; mix well and pour into prepared can or mold. Place 2 paper towels on top of can to absorb condensation; cover tightly with aluminum foil. Set can in slow cooker; pour about 2 inches of water around can. Cover and cook on high setting for 5 to 6 hours. Let cool 10 minutes; turn pudding out of can. Slice and serve.

Steamed Cranberry Pudding

Pumpkin Butter

Laura Williams, *Evansville, TN*

Pumpkin Butter

My husband calls this "Pumpkin Pie in a Jar." If you don't have fresh pumpkin, you can substitute a 15-ounce can of pumpkin. You can easily double or triple this recipe. It's wonderful to keep on hand for making homemade pumpkin pies or bread.

Makes about four 1/2-pint jars

2 c. fresh pumpkin, cooked and puréed
1 c. sugar
1 c. brown sugar, packed
1 t. cinnamon
1/4 t. nutmeg
1/2 t. ginger
1/8 t. ground cloves
4 1/2-pint canning jars and lids, sterilized

Combine all ingredients in a slow cooker; mix well. Cover and cook on high setting for 3 hours, stirring occasionally to prevent scorching. It will thicken as it cooks. Ladle hot mixture into hot sterilized jars, leaving 1/4-inch headspace. Wipe rims; secure with lids and rings. Process in a boiling water bath for 40 minutes or pressure canner at 10 pounds of pressure for 20 minutes. Set jars on a towel to cool; check for seals.

Angie McCabe, *Monticello, IL*

Apple Spice Cake

Warm apple spice cake makes the whole house smell like grandma's kitchen on a cold fall day...mmm!

Serves 8

21-oz. can apple pie filling
18-1/4 oz. pkg. spice cake mix
1/2 c. butter
Garnish: vanilla ice cream

Spray a slow cooker generously with non-stick vegetable spray. Spread pie filling in slow cooker; sprinkle evenly with dry cake mix. Do not stir. Dot with butter. Cover and cook on high setting for 2 to 3 hours, until center has risen and edges are bubbly. Spoon into individual bowls; serve warm, topped with ice cream.

Vickie, *Gooseberry Patch*

Vickie's Chocolate Fondue

Delicious dipping for squares of pound cake, mandarin oranges, cherries and strawberries!

Makes 2-1/2 cups

24-oz. pkg. semi-sweet chocolate chips
1 pt. whipping cream
6 T. corn syrup
6 T. orange extract

Melt chocolate chips in the top of a double boiler; add remaining ingredients and stir to blend. When fondue is warm, spoon into a fondue pot or small slow cooker on low heat to keep sauce warm.

Penny Sherman, *Ava, MO*

Streusel-Topped Coffee Cake

Share this tender cake with friends before setting off for a day of Christmas shopping.

Makes 8 servings

1-3/4 c. biscuit baking mix, divided
3/4 c. sugar
1/2 c. vanilla yogurt
1 egg, beaten
1 t. vanilla extract
1/4 c. brown sugar, packed
1/2 t. cinnamon
1/2 c. powdered sugar
1 to 2 T. milk

Coat a slow cooker with non-stick vegetable spray. Cut a circle of parchment paper to fit the bottom of the crock; press into place and spray again. In a bowl, mix 1-1/2 cups biscuit mix, sugar, yogurt, egg and vanilla until well blended; set aside. In a small bowl, mix brown sugar, cinnamon and remaining biscuit mix. Spoon half of batter into slow cooker; sprinkle half of brown sugar mixture on top. Repeat layers. Place 2 paper towels on top of slow cooker to absorb condensation. Cover and cook on high setting for 1-3/4 to 2 hours, until a toothpick inserted in the center tests clean. Let coffee cake stand in crock for 10 minutes. Turn out onto a plate; peel off parchment paper. Turn cake over again onto a serving platter, so streusel is on top. In a separate small bowl, whisk together powdered sugar and milk, adding enough milk to form a drizzling consistency. Drizzle glaze over coffee cake.

Carrie O'Shea, *Marina Del Rey, CA*

Peanut Butter Fudge

This yummy fudge is a perfect holiday gift for the ones you love.

Serves 15

3 c. peanut butter chips and/or semi-sweet chocolate chips
14-oz. can sweetened condensed milk
1 t. vanilla extract
1 t. butter
3/4 c. creamy peanut butter
Optional: 1/2 c. chopped nuts

Spray a 4-quart slow-cooker with non-stick vegetable spray. Add all ingredients to slow cooker; mix gently. Cover and cook on low setting for 2 hours, stirring occasionally. Spread fudge into a parchment paper-lined rimmed baking sheet. Refrigerate until firm, about 4 hours. Cut into squares and serve.

Slow-Cooker Peanut Butter Fudge

Giant Chocolate Chip Cookie

Cheri Maxwell, *Gulf Breeze, FL*

Giant Chocolate Chip Cookie

My dad loves cookies and this giant cookie recipe put a huge smile on his face for Father's Day!

Serves 10

2/3 c. butter, softened
2/3 c. light brown sugar, packed
3/4 c. plus 2 T. superfine sugar
2 eggs
1 T. vanilla extract
1 c. all-purpose flour
1/2 t. baking powder
1/4 t. salt
2/3 c. semi-sweet or dark chocolate chips

Line the bottom of a 7-quart slow cooker with parchment paper; grease paper and set aside. In a large bowl, beat together butter, sugars, eggs and vanilla until fluffy. In a separate bowl, stir together flour, baking powder and salt. Add flour mixture to butter mixture; knead into dough. Fold in chocolate chips. Spoon dough into slow cooker; press it evenly into the bottom. Cover and cook on low setting for 2 to 3 hours. During the last 30 minutes, open the lid slightly; turn to high setting and cook for final 30 minutes. Remove crock to a wire rack; let cool for 30 minutes. Carefully turn cookie out onto a wire rack. Cool completely; cut into wedges.

Joyce Stackhouse, *Cadiz, OH*

Warm Mocha Cake

This is such a comforting dessert on a cold autumn day. I like to serve it with a scoop of vanilla ice cream or fresh whipped cream. It also makes the house smell amazing while it's cooking away...I hope you enjoy it as much as we do!

Serves 8

1 c. all-purpose flour
2/3 c. light brown sugar, packed
1/2 c. baking cocoa, divided
1/4 t. baking soda
1/4 t. salt
1/2 c. milk
1 T. butter, melted
1 t. vanilla extract
3/4 c. sugar
1-1/3 c. hot water
2 T. instant coffee granules

Preheat a lightly greased slow cooker on high setting. In a bowl, combine flour, brown sugar, 1/4 cup cocoa, baking soda, salt, milk, butter and vanilla; mix until smooth. Spoon batter into a lightly greased slow cooker. In a bowl, combine sugar and remaining cocoa; sprinkle over batter. Combine hot water and coffee granules; stir until granules are dissolved. Drizzle coffee mixture over all; do not stir. Cover and cook on high setting for 2 hours. Remove crock from heat to a wire rack; let cool 15 minutes before serving.

Slow-Cooker Apple Pie

Diana Krol, *Nickerson, KS*

Slow-Cooker Apple Pie

This is a wonderful dessert to take to potluck dinners or tailgating parties...especially in the fall when the apples are at their peak.

Serves 8 to 10

8 c. apples, peeled, cored and sliced
1-1/4 t. cinnamon
1/4 t. nutmeg
2 eggs, beaten
3/4 c. milk
2 t. vanilla extract
3/4 c. sugar
5 T. butter, softened and divided
1-1/2 c. biscuit baking mix, divided
1/3 c. brown sugar, packed
Garnish: whipped cream or vanilla ice cream

In a large bowl, toss together apples, cinnamon and nutmeg; transfer to a greased slow cooker. In a bowl, blend eggs, milk, vanilla, sugar, 2 tablespoons butter and 3/4 cup baking mix. Spoon batter over apples. In a small bowl, combine brown sugar and remaining baking mix; cut in remaining butter until mixture resembles coarse crumbs. Spoon brown sugar mixture over batter. Do not stir. Cover and cook on low setting for 6 to 7 hours. Serve warm, spooned into individual bowls and topped with whipped cream or ice cream.

Kay Marone, *Des Moines, IA*

Chocolate Mocha Bread Pudding

It's the perfect dessert if you love coffee or chocolate...or both!

Serves 8 to 10

1 loaf hearty white bread, cubed
4 c. milk
1/4 c. whipping cream
6 eggs, beaten
1 T. vanilla extract
1 c. sugar
1 c. brown sugar, packed
1/4 c. baking cocoa
1 T. instant espresso powder
1 c. semi-sweet chocolate chips

Spray a large slow cooker with non-stick vegetable spray. Place bread cubes in slow cooker. In a bowl, whisk together milk, cream, eggs and vanilla. In a separate bowl, combine sugars, cocoa and espresso powder; add to milk mixture, stirring well. Pour milk mixture over bread cubes. Stir and press bread cubes into milk mixture until they are fully coated. Sprinkle with chocolate chips. Cover and cook on high setting for 2 to 3 hours, until set.

Vickie, *Gooseberry Patch*

Pumpkin-Walnut Pie Pudding

Pumpkin pie is my favorite kind of pie, but sometimes you just want something a little bit different. When I tried this recipe, I liked it almost as much as regular pumpkin pie!

Serves 8

15-oz. can pumpkin
5-oz. can evaporated milk
1/3 c. sugar
2 T. pumpkin pie spice, divided
9-oz. pkg. yellow cake mix
1 c. walnuts, toasted and chopped
1/4 c. butter, melted
Garnish: whipped topping

In a bowl, mix together pumpkin, milk, sugar and one tablespoon spice. Spread pumpkin mixture in a lightly greased slow cooker; set aside. In a bowl, combine dry cake mix, walnuts and remaining spice; sprinkle evenly over pumpkin mixture. Drizzle melted butter over all. Cover and cook on high setting for 2-1/2 hours. Remove crock from slow cooker and set on a wire rack to cool slightly. Spoon pudding into serving bowls; top with a dollop of whipped topping.

Amy Butcher, *Columbus, GA*

Perfectly Poached Pears

This delectable dessert looks like you spent hours making it, but it'll be your little secret that the slow cooker did most of the work! Use red wine for a grown-up dessert, grape juice if you'll be serving to children.

Serves 6 to 8

6 pears, peeled, halved and cored
3 c. red wine or grape juice
1 c. sugar
1 t. vanilla extract
4-inch cinnamon stick
2 whole star anise pods
Garnish: whipped cream

Place pears in a slow cooker. Drizzle wine or grape juice over pears. Gently stir in sugar until it dissolves, being careful not to break up pear halves. Stir in vanilla; add cinnamon stick and whole star anise pods. Cover and cook on low setting for 5 hours. Remove pears to serving bowls with a slotted spoon. Discard whole spices. Serve pears topped with a dollop of whipped cream, drizzled with a little sauce from slow cooker.

Perfectly Poached Pears

Fall-Favorite Apple Coffee Cake

Jen Licon-Conner, *Gooseberry Patch*

Fall-Favorite Apple Coffee Cake

This is one of my favorite things to make with all the apples I get from our local orchard. Every year I go and buy so many apples and a few gallons of apple cider...a cherished tradition.

Serves 8

2 c. biscuit baking mix
2/3 c. applesauce
1/4 c. milk
2 T. sugar
2 T. butter, softened
2 apples, peeled, cored and diced
1 t. cinnamon
1 t. vanilla extract
1 egg, lightly beaten

In a large bowl, combine all ingredients; mix well. Spoon batter into a lightly greased slow cooker; sprinkle with Crumbly Cinnamon Topping. Cover and cook on high setting for 2-1/2 to 3 hours, until a toothpick inserted in the center of cake tests clean. Uncover and remove crock to a wire rack to cool. Loosen sides of cake with a thin spatula; remove cake and slice to serve.

Crumbly Cinnamon Topping:

1/4 c. biscuit baking mix
1/4 c. brown sugar, packed
1 t. cinnamon
1/4 c. chopped walnuts
2 T. butter, chilled

Combine all ingredients except butter in a bowl. Cut in butter with a pastry blender or 2 forks until crumbly.

Joanne Mello, *North Dartmouth, MA*

Harvest Indian Pudding

I live in New England, and every Thanksgiving I make this special dessert that's reminiscent of the first Thanksgiving in Plymouth, Massachusetts.

Serves 6 to 8

3 c. milk
1/2 c. cornmeal
1/2 t. salt
3 eggs
1/4 c. light brown sugar, packed
1/3 c. molasses
2 T. butter
1/2 t. cinnamon
1/4 t. allspice
1/2 t. ground ginger
Garnish: vanilla ice cream

Preheat a lightly greased slow cooker on high setting for 20 minutes. Meanwhile, combine milk, cornmeal and salt in a saucepan over medium heat. Bring milk mixture to a boil. Cook, stirring constantly, for 5 minutes. Reduce heat, cover and simmer for 10 minutes. Combine eggs and remaining ingredients except ice cream in a bowl; mix well. Slowly whisk milk mixture into egg mixture; whisk until smooth. Pour batter into preheated slow cooker. Cover and cook on high setting for 2 to 3 hours, or on low setting for 6 to 8 hours. Serve pudding with a scoop of ice cream.

Hope Comerford, *Clinton Township, MI*

Eggnog Bread Pudding

This bread pudding has the delicious flavor of eggnog and just a hint of the yummy liqueur I soak the raisins in! It isn't too sweet, but just sweet enough. This recipe feeds lots of people, so halve it if you're cooking for a smaller gathering.

Serves 15 to 20

2 loaves French bread
1 c. raisins
Optional: 1/2 c. Mexican coffee-flavored
  vodka-based liqueur
8 eggs, beaten
2 t. vanilla extract
1/4 t. ground nutmeg
1/2 t. salt
1/4 c. butter, melted
1 c. sugar
4 c. eggnog
Garnish: whipped cream

The day before preparing bread pudding, cut bread loaves into cubes and spread out to dry. The next day, soak raisins in liqueur, if using, until plump. Meanwhile, mix eggs, vanilla, nutmeg and salt in a very large bowl. Stir in butter, sugar and eggnog. Mix well. Add raisins, with or without liqueur; stir well. Slowly fold in dry bread cubes, stirring until all cubes are coated with egg mixture. Transfer mixture to a large slow cooker that has been sprayed with non-stick vegetable spray. Cover and cook on low setting for 4 to 6 hours, until a knife tip tests clean when inserted into the center. During the last hour of cooking time, place 2 paper towels under the lid to keep the top from getting soggy. Serve warm, topped with whipped cream.

Carol Smith, *West Lawn, PA*

Scalloped Pineapple

It isn't a potluck to us until someone brings the Scalloped Pineapple! It's so good with ice cream.

Makes 8 servings

1 c. sugar
3 eggs, beaten
3/4 c. butter, melted
3/4 c. milk
20-oz. can crushed pineapple, drained
8 slices bread, cubed
Garnish: vanilla ice cream

Mix all ingredients except ice cream in a slow cooker. Cover and cook on high setting for 2 hours. Reduce heat to low; cook for one additional hour. Garnish portions with scoops of ice cream.

Scalloped Pineapple

Index

Index

U.S. to Metric Recipe Equivalents

Volume Measurements

¼ teaspoon	1 mL
½ teaspoon	2 mL
1 teaspoon	5 mL
1 tablespoon = 3 teaspoons	15 mL
2 tablespoons = 1 fluid ounce	30 mL
¼ cup	60 mL
⅓ cup	75 mL
½ cup = 4 fluid ounces	125 mL
1 cup = 8 fluid ounces	250 mL
2 cups = 1 pint = 16 fluid ounces	500 mL
4 cups = 1 quart	1 L

Weights

1 ounce	30 g
4 ounces	120 g
8 ounces	225 g
16 ounces = 1 pound	450 g

Baking Pan Sizes

Square

8x8x2 inches	2 L = 20x20x5 cm
9x9x2 inches	2.5 L = 23x23x5 cm

Rectangular

13x9x2 inches	3.5 L = 33x23x5 cm

Loaf

9x5x3 inches	2 L = 23x13x7 cm

Round

8x1-½ inches	1.2 L = 20x4 cm
9x1-½ inches	1.5 L = 23x4 cm

Recipe Abbreviations

t. = teaspoon	ltr. = liter
T. = tablespoon	oz. = ounce
c. = cup	lb. = pound
pt. = pint	doz. = dozen
qt. = quart	pkg. = package
gal. = gallon	env. = envelope

Oven Temperatures

300° F	150° C
325° F	160° C
350° F	180° C
375° F	190° C
400° F	200° C
450° F	230° C

Kitchen Measurements

A pinch = ⅛ tablespoon
1 fluid ounce = 2 tablespoons
3 teaspoons = 1 tablespoon
4 fluid ounces = ½ cup
2 tablespoons = ⅛ cup
8 fluid ounces = 1 cup
4 tablespoons = ¼ cup
16 fluid ounces = 1 pint
8 tablespoons = ½ cup
32 fluid ounces = 1 quart
16 tablespoons = 1 cup
16 ounces net weight = 1 pound
2 cups = 1 pint
4 cups = 1 quart
4 quarts = 1 gallon

Send us your favorite recipe

and the memory that makes it special for you!*

....

If we select your recipe for a brand-new **Gooseberry Patch** cookbook,
your name will appear right along with it...and you'll receive a
FREE copy of the book!

Submit your recipe on our website at
www.gooseberrypatch.com/sharearecipe

*Please include the number of servings and all other necessary information.

Have a taste for more?

Visit www.gooseberrypatch.com to join our Circle of Friends!

....

- • Free recipes, tips and ideas plus a complete cookbook index
- • Get special email offers and our monthly eLetter delivered to your inbox

From our Kitchen to Yours

You'll also love these cookbooks from **Gooseberry Patch**!

150 Backyard Cookout Recipes

150 Recipes in a 13x9 Pan

5-Ingredient Family Favorite Recipes

Church Suppers

Best-Ever Cookie, Brownie & Bar Recipes

Busy-Day Slow Cooking

Comfort Food Lightened Up

Delicious Recipes for Diabetics

Easy Classic Casseroles

Farmhouse Christmas

Homestyle in a Hurry

America's Comfort Foods

Soups, Stews & Breads

Tasty Fall Cooking

www.gooseberrypatch.com